W. J Wintle

Armenia and its Sorrows

W. J Wintle

Armenia and its Sorrows

ISBN/EAN: 9783337288624

Printed in Europe, USA, Canada, Australia, Japan

Cover: Foto ©ninafisch / pixelio.de

More available books at **www.hansebooks.com**

ARMENIA

AND ITS SORROWS

By W. J. WINTLE

AUTHOR OF
"THE STORY OF FLORENCE NIGHTINGALE" ETC.

THIRD EDITION

With an Additional Chapter, bringing the record down to
September 1896

> "That such things should be done once is a damning disgrace to the portion of our race which did them; that a door should be left open for their ever-so-barely possible repetition would spread that shame over the whole."
> — W. E. GLADSTONE.

LONDON:
ANDREW MELROSE
16 PILGRIM STREET, E.C.

To the Memory of
SCHAKHE
THE WIFE OF GRGO
AND MANY OTHER WOMEN OF SASSOUN
WHO
AFTER FIGHTING IN SELF-DEFENCE FOR TWENTY-FOUR HOURS
CAST THEMSELVES OVER A PRECIPICE,
CHOOSING RATHER
TO PASS UNBIDDEN TO THE PRESENCE
OF
THE ALL-PITIFUL FATHER
THAN TO FALL INTO THE HANDS OF THE TURK
THIS BOOK IS DEDICATED

PREFACE.

THE following work, undertaken at the Publisher's suggestion, is an attempt to present, within the limits of a small book, a concise but comprehensive account of the Armenians and their recent sufferings. If it be thought that the description of the outrages is unduly ghastly, I can, but say that I have suppressed more than I have published. In all cases my information has been derived from the official reports of British representatives, or from other sources of unquestionable veracity. I am indebted to the courtesy of Messrs. Hodder & Stoughton for permission to quote from the Rev. F. D. Greene's *Armenian Crisis*, to Canon MacColl, Dr. E. J. Dillon, and the Editor of the *Contemporary Review* for permission to use recent articles on the subject, and to Mr. William Watson and his Publisher, Mr. John Lane, for leave to reprint a sonnet from *The Purple East*.

W. J. W.

August 31st, 1896.

NOTE TO SECOND EDITION.

THE first edition having been exhausted in less than three weeks, a second now becomes necessary. Unhappily another wholesale massacre has taken place within this short space of time, and I have now the painful task of bringing the book up to date by the addition of an Appendix dealing with the recent horrors in Constantinople. My thanks are due to the public for the kindly reception which has been accorded to the book.

W. J. W.

September 18th, 1896.

CONTENTS.

CHAP.		PAGE
I.	DESCRIPTION OF THE COUNTRY	9
II.	HISTORY OF THE NATION	22
III.	THE PEOPLE AND THEIR LANGUAGE	32
IV.	THE CHURCH IN ARMENIA	42
V.	THE ORIGINS OF TROUBLE	49
VI.	THE SASSOUN MASSACRE AND THE COMMISSION OF INQUIRY	64
VII.	THE WORK OF EXTERMINATION	83
VIII.	EUROPE'S RESPONSIBILITY	99
	APPENDIX	113

LIST OF ILLUSTRATIONS.

MAP OF ASIATIC TURKEY	
MASSACRE OF ARMENIANS AT CONSTANTINOPLE	*Frontispiece*
	PAGE
ARMENIAN MONASTERY AT VARAK	15
ABDUL HAMID II.	27
ARMENIAN PEASANT WOMEN	37
ARMENIAN EX-PATRIARCH OF CONSTANTINOPLE	45
KURDISH MOUNTAINEERS	57
ARMENIAN MOUNTAINEER	73
THE CEMETERY AT ERZEROUM	85
TREBIZOND	89
SIR PHILIP CURRIE	103

HOW LONG?

Heaped in their ghastly graves they lie, the breeze
Sickening o'er fields where others vainly wait
For burial: and the butchers keep high state
In silken palaces of perfumed ease.
The panther of the desert, matched with these,
Is pitiful; beside their lust and hate,
Fire and the plague-wind are compassionate,
And soft the deadliest fangs of ravening seas.

How long shall they be borne? Is not the cup
Of crime yet full? Doth devildom still lack
Some consummating crown, that we hold back
The scourge, and in Christ's borders give them room?
How long shall they be borne, O England! Up,
Tempest of God, and sweep them to their doom!

—*William Watson.*

From "The Purple East" (John Lane)
by special permission.

ARMENIA AND ITS SORROWS.

CHAPTER I.

DESCRIPTION OF THE COUNTRY.

ARMENIA occupies a position unique among the nations of the earth. The native traditions claim that its mountain fastnesses and fertile valleys were the home of earth's first inhabitants, that the flowers of Eden blossomed in its meadows when the world was young, and that on its lonely uplands the ark of Noah rested. Lying almost central between three continents, it has been the fatherland of mighty peoples, and from its early annals have flowed broad streams of human history.

It occupies a prominent position in the history both of the world and of Christianity. It was the fighting ground for Medes and Persians, Greeks and Babylonians, Turks and Russians. Its language takes us back to the days of the cuneiform inscriptions, and the methods of the patriarchs still survive in its agricultural operations. Its ancient Church preserves the doctrines and the ritual of the sub-apostolic age, and it glories in the fact that the light of Christianity has never gone out in the land. Its muster-roll of martyrs and confessors is unique. No Christian Church under heaven has endured such unremitting persecution. For many months past, the whole civilised world has echoed with the long-drawn wail of agony which has gone up to God from tortured children, from dying men, and from outraged women. The fell shadow of the False Prophet has hung like a pall upon the land, and the darkness thickens even while we write.

Occupying the greater part of the triangle which lies between three seas,—the Caspian, the Euxine, and the Mediterranean,—Armenia consists of an elevated country, ranging from four to seven thousand feet above the level of the sea. It is between four and five hundred miles long, and is about the same in breadth, stretching from the Caucasus on the north to Kurdistan on the south, and from the Caspian Sea on the east to Asia Minor on the west.

It was anciently divided into two parts: Armenia Major on the east of the Euphrates, and Armenia Minor to the west. The northern portion is now governed by Russia, and a small corner on the south-east is owned by Persia, but the largest part still groans beneath the blundering despotism of the Ottoman Empire.

The country consists mainly of pastoral plateaus, traversed by picturesque chains of hills, which culminate in the snow-capped peaks of Ararat, towering heavenward almost seventeen thousand feet. These mountains are composed of volcanic rock, and the peaks still retain the form of craters, but ancient history affords us no records of their activity, though a German writer stated that in 1783 he saw smoke and fire emitted from one of them—a statement for which there is not, however, any corroboration.

The volcanic nature of the country is clearly

indicated, not only by the geological formations, but by the presence of numerous hot sulphur and mineral springs, as also by the occurrence of disastrous earthquakes. In 1840 the village of Aicuri was entirely destroyed and about a thousand people buried alive, while in Erevan and Nakhjevan hundreds of houses were overthrown. Three years later, Erzeroum was visited with a similar calamity, and as lately as 1891, volcanic disturbances were reported in the district of Van.

Six great rivers have their sources in the highlands of Armenia,—the Euphrates, the Tigris, the Araxes, the Cyrus, the Acampsis, and the Halys,—and flow into three separate seas, fertilising the valleys as they go. The Tigris has been identified with the Biblical Hiddekel, and the Acampsis is supposed to be the Pison, while many students of antiquity consider the Araxes to be the ancient Gihon.

The national tradition that the human race had its origin in Armenia we cannot here discuss. It may, however, be not unreasonably asked, whether the country still possesses any traces of that abounding fertility and primal beauty with which tradition clothes it. An eloquent Armenian writer thus answers the inquiry:—

"Her natural beauty, salubrious climate, her exuberant fertility, the fragrance of her flowers, the variety of her singing birds, above all, her mountainous bosom and overflowing breasts from which the mighty waters run down on her sides and fill the great channels of those rivers, which fertilise the subjacent countries and replenish the three adjacent seas; all these do justify her claim. . . . If variety makes beauty, Armenia furnishes such a variety, making her one of the most beautiful countries in the world; not only has she those gigantic mountains with their snow-crowned heads looking down upon the clouds that envelop their skirts, while they mock at the ambient air and the winds; not only has she hundreds of murmuring streams and rippling brooks gliding along the sides of thousands of hills, which swell those kingly rivers and cause them to overflow their banks; but she also has some beautiful lakes, like jewels set in their respective caskets."

The Hon. Robert Curzon, in his work on Armenia, wrote enthusiastically of the lovely flowers of the country. "Though one of them has a Latin scientific name, no plant of it has ever been in Europe, and by no manner of contrivance could we succeed in carrying one away. This most beautiful production was called in Turkish, 'Seven brothers' blood,' and in Latin *Philipea coccinea*. It is a parasite on absinthe, or wormwood. This is the most beautiful flower conceivable: it is in the form of a lily, about nine to twelve inches long, including the stalk; the flower, and stalk, and all parts of it resembling crimson velvet; it has no leaves; it is found on the sides of the mountains near Erzeroum, often in company with the *Morena Orientalis*, a remarkable kind of thistle, with flowers all up the stalk, looking and smelling like the honeysuckle. Another beautiful flower found here has not been described. It grows among rocks, and has a tough carroty root, two feet or more in length; the leaves are long grassy filaments, forming a low bush, like a tussock of coarse grass: under the leaves appear the flowers. Each plant has twelve or twenty of them, like large white-heart cherries on a stalk, in the form of a bunch of grapes, eight or ten inches long; these flowers are merely coloured bladders holding the seed. An iris, of a most brilliant flaming yellow, is found among the rocks, and it, as well as all the more remarkable flowers of this country, blooms in the spring soon after the melting of the snow—that is to say, about June."

The general aspect of the country is varied in the extreme, the fertility of the sheltered valleys contrasting strongly with the rugged bareness of the wind-swept hills. The road between Erzeroum and Trebizond is especially noted for its beauty.

After passing the summit, bare, down-like hills surround the traveller, and then beautiful spruce-fir forests fill the gorge, while the ground beneath them is a tangle of rhododendrons. Even in mid-winter the scenery here is very lovely, and in spring, when the rhododendrons are in flower, and the spruce, beech, and other trees in full leaf, simply perfect. Villages soon come into sight, and detached houses begin to dot the hillside; green grass stretches in glades by the riverside, while every available spot on the hills is under cultivation. Here and there, near a village, where fir trees do not hide the view, the sides of the ravine may be seen rising often in sheer precipices for hundreds of feet, terminating high up in the clouds in rugged peaks and crags, on some of which may be seen the ruins of old stone castles. Wherever on the cliff a tree can find root, there stands a tall tapering spruce, or a dense patch of rhododendrons. In some parts wear and tear, a shock of earthquake, or a flash of lightning, has rent a rocky summit and toppled the greater part of it down the face of the hill, where masses as big as cathedrals remain, looking as if the push of a hand would send them rolling on. Some of these rocks have fallen into the brook, completely blocking its course, and the water has risen behind them till it reached the top and now comes rushing over in a pretty cascade.

Mr. H. C. Barkley's description of another type of Armenian scenery is very notable. "It was a morning that may be seen for months together in the land of the Turk, but rarely indeed in western Europe. The great undulating plains, that would look burnt up, bare, and desolate under the blaze of the noonday sun, were now bathed in a soft creamy light. Above the river and ravines fleecy clouds hung suspended, the light from the rising sun tinting them and the shadows they cast with indescribably beautiful colours, which changed and changed again each minute.

"Picturesque groups of Turks, on horseback or on foot, moved slowly from the town in all directions to their work in the fields, while by the side of the road some score of men and women, oxen and horses, were busy on a threshing-floor—the animals trampling out the corn, the men and women tossing and sifting the grain from the chaff. Then, in mid-distance, emerging from the river mists, came a long string of camels, with their bright trappings and heavy loads, stalking along in their slow, weird manner, the sound of their pretty tinkling bells growing louder and louder, while the cloud of yellow dust raised by their feet mixed with the morning mists and enhanced the rich beauty of the scene. But, alas! this beauty did not last long, or rather our enjoyment of it was soon over, for on reaching the summit of a steep rise the sun shone painfully hot in our faces, and at the same time a breeze, coming up from behind, soon enveloped us in a thick cloud of dust that shut out the view. We felt that the pleasant but short morning was past, the world was fairly awake, and before us lay a long road and a weary journey. Soon human and animal life almost altogether disappeared, and we were the only moving things on the dreary, burnt-up waste. Hour after hour we pressed onward, the day getting hotter and the country less interesting."

One of the most remarkable features of the country

ARMENIAN MONASTERY, VARAK, NEAR VAN.

is Lake Van. It is ninety miles long and thirty broad, and its area is about twice as large as that of the Lake of Geneva. Although buried deep in the midst of lofty mountains, it is yet more than five thousand feet above the level of the sea. It has no outlet, and its waters are very salt.

When the traveller reaches the crest of the hills, a landscape of surprising beauty awaits him. At his feet, intensely blue and glittering in the rays of the sun, lies the inland sea with the peak of the Subban Dagh mirrored in its transparent waters. The city of Van, with its castle-crowned rock and its embattled walls and towers, lies surrounded by orchards and gardens. On the right, a rugged snow-capped mountain opens midway into an amphitheatre, in which, amid lofty trees, stands the Armenian Convent of Seven Churches. To the west of the lake is the Nimrod Dagh, and the highlands containing the sources of the great rivers of Mesopotamia. The hills forming the foreground of the picture are carpeted with the brightest flowers, over which wander the flocks, while gaily-dressed shepherds gather around.

The climate of Armenia is as varied as the general aspect of the country. A region of heavy rains, with subtropical heat, will be found in the valley of the Kur, extending from Tiflis to the Caspian Sea, and in the valley of the Upper Tigris, while the opposite extreme of perpetual snow prevails in the higher districts of Ararat. Between these extremes, every kind of climate may be experienced; the higher tablelands being as a rule bleak and barren, while the more sheltered valleys are warm and fertile. The plateaus, which are volcanic, dry, and generally destitute of trees, have long and inclement winters, lasting from the middle of October until the beginning of May, when a brief, hot summer follows. The country suffers much from the cold north winds, against which it has no protection; and these, meeting the south and east winds, give rise to the storms which render the navigation of the Black Sea coast so dangerous.

During the long and bitter winter, however bright the sky may be, the sun's rays give little heat, and only pain the eyes with the glare upon the snow. This glare has a very marked effect, sometimes bringing on a blindness called snow-blindness, and raising blisters on the face precisely like those which are produced by exposure to extreme heat. Another inconvenience is somewhat absurd: the breath, out of doors, congeals upon the moustaches and beard, and speedily produces icicles, which prevent the possibility of opening the mouth. Those who wear long beards are sometimes obliged to commence the series of Turkish civilities in dumb show; their faces being fixtures for the time, they are not able to speak till their beards thaw. A curious phenomenon may also be sometimes observed upon the door of one of the subterranean stables being opened, when, although the day is clear and fine without, the warm air within immediately congeals into a little fall of snow; this may be seen in great perfection on the first opening of the outer door in the morning, when the house is warm from its having been shut up all night.

At the melting of the snow the wolves often come even into the towns, and devour the dogs, which are everywhere numerous. There are gruesome stories of their carrying off the little peeping children, who creep out of the houses at the beginning of spring, and who are occasionally washed away in the torrents of melted snow. Wolves are not very infrequently started out of the inside of one of the many dead horses whose wornout bodies have been frozen as hard as flint during the winter, and which form savoury banquets for the famished wolves when the snow and ice recede, and display these dainty morsels to their eager eyes.

During great part of the winter the cold is so severe that anyone standing still for any length of time is in great danger of being frozen to death. Dead frozen bodies are frequently brought into the towns : and it is common, on the melting of the snow, to find numerous corpses of men and bodies of horses who have perished during the winter.

Let it never be forgotten that it was in a winter such as we have described that Turkish savagery drove forth hundreds of women and little children to wander, starving and half naked, until the drifting snow became their winding-sheet.

The vegetation of Armenia is fairly abundant, when the shortness of the summer is taken into account. The richest belt of vegetation is found in the broad valley of the Aras ; but the marshes produced by the many irrigating channels make this the most malarious district in the whole country. The highlands are chiefly pastoral, though a little corn is cultivated ; but the valleys support rich vineyards and orchards, fields of cotton, rice, flax, hemp, and tobacco.

The natural history of the country is interesting, the bear, lynx, and wolf being the principal wild beasts. The lemming, jerboa, and marmot are common, while the fox, beaver, and grey badger are only occasionally seen. Wild sheep are fairly numerous in the mountains, and are said to be even more difficult of approach than the chamois of the Alps, while the capricorn is another difficult capture.

In bygone days the Armenian horses were as famed as the Arab steeds are now, and we read that the rich pastures of the country provided excellent mounts for the Medo-Persian army. We have an allusion to this fact in Ezekiel xxvii. 14 : "They of the house of

Togarmah [Armenia] traded for thy wares with horses and war-horses and mules."

At the present time the camel is largely used in Armenia as a beast of burden. Cattle and sheep are domesticated widely, but the severity of the climate has produced very stunted breeds. The birds of the country are singularly numerous. Such flocks of sheldrakes and wild geese settle down in the plains that sometimes the surface of the ground is completely hidden. Herons, cranes, and storks abound, and quails are said to be as thick as flies. Mr. Calvert, when at Erzeroum, noted no less than a hundred and sixty-eight species of wild birds in the immediate district. It may amuse the reader to peruse the following specimen of Armenian folk-lore, which claims to give us the origin of the domestic goose:—

"In former times two geese, agreed to take a long journey together. The evening before they were to set out one said to the other, 'Mind you are ready, my friend, for, Inshallah! I shall set out to-morrow morning.' The other replied, 'And so will I, whether it pleases God or not.' The sun rose next morning, and the pious goose, having eaten his breakfast and quenched his thirst in the waters of the stream, rose lightly on the wing, and soared away to a distant land. The profane bird also prepared to follow him, but after hopping and fluttering for a long while, he found himself totally unable to rise from the ground, and being observed by a passing fowler, was presently caught and reduced to servitude, in which his race have ever since continued, while the descendants of the pious goose still enjoy their original freedom."

The mineral resources of Armenia are very extensive. Traces of old gold mines have been found near Erzeroum, and there are rich copper and silver mines in the neighbourhood of Harpoot, the former being said to yield annually about two million two hundred and fifty thousand pounds. There are also mines of antimony, sulphur, and sulphuret of lead. Coal and iron are abundant, but the former is totally neglected, and the iron mines are little worked. At Divrig, masses of native iron are found, and are roughly shaped into tools by the villagers.

There can be little doubt that immense wealth awaits the man or Government who shall develop the mineral resources of this country.

CHAPTER II.

HISTORY OF THE NATION.

ACCORDING to the national traditions, the Armenians are the descendants of Haik, the son of Togarmah, the grandson of Japhet. The historians of the country frequently call the people by the appellation of "Torgomian Doon," the house of Togarmah, and the same expression is used by the prophet Ezekiel. This tradition is regarded as highly probable by the best authorities.

Professor Delitzsch, in his *Commentary on Genesis*, says: "The Armenians regarded Thorgom (Togarmah), the father of Haik, as their ancestor; and even granting that the form of the name Thorgom was occasioned by Thorgama of the Septuagint, still the Armenian tradition is confirmed by *Tilgarimmu* being in the cuneiform inscription the name of a fortified town in the subsequent district of Melitene, on the south-western boundary of Armenia."

Professor Rawlinson, whose authority on such subjects no one will dispute, says: "Grimm's view that Togarmah is composed of two elements—*Toka*, which in Sanskrit means a tribe or race, and *Armah* (Armenia)—may well be accepted. The Armenian tradition which derives the Haikian race from Thorgom, as it can scarcely be a coincidence, must be regarded as having considerable value. Now, the existing Armenians, the legitimate descendants of those who occupied the country in the time of Ezekiel, speak a language which modern ethnologists pronounce to be decidedly Indo-European; and thus, so far, modern science confirms the scriptural account."

We condense the following sketch of the tradition in question, from the account given by a native writer, Dr. Gabrielian.

About B.C. 2350, Haik, the son of Togarmah, was in search of a suitable locality in which to settle. In company with his relatives, he descended into the plain of Shinar, in Mesopotamia. Here the people, fearing another flood, commenced to build the Tower of Babel, and the family of Haik distinguished themselves by wisdom and virtue in this enterprise. But ambitious Belus, desiring the supremacy, and even demanding that his image should be reverenced, became obnoxious to the other tribes. Haik and his sons therefore returned to their native place in the land of Ararat, close by the lake of Van.

Belus speedily pursued them with a strong force, but after a sanguinary conflict, he was killed by an arrow shot by Haik, and his army dispersed. Haik, after this, lived to a great age, founded towns and villages, and died in peace. From that day till this, his descendants have called themselves *Haiks*, and their country *Haiasdan*.

Haik was succeeded by his son Armenag, from whose name some suppose the word Armenia to have been derived, and after him came, in succession, Aramais, Amassia, Harmah, and Aram. This last monarch is credited with having driven out the Babylonian and Median invaders, and is said to have subdued large districts west of the Euphrates.

After the death of Aram, the country slowly sank into a subordinate condition to the Assyrians, though kings of the Haikian dynasty continued to rule over the land, but with greatly diminished prestige.

Passing over the dim, uncertain centuries during which the nation was more or less subject to the Assyrians, having been completely conquered by Semiramis, and regaining a certain degree of independence under Sardanapalus, we arrive at the period of Tigranes I., who was contemporary with Cyrus, the Persian monarch. These kings are represented by Xenophon as being on terms of intimate friendship. It is interesting to note that the Armenian nation, under the name of Ararat, is represented by Jeremiah (li. 27) as uniting with the Medes to destroy Babylon: "Prepare the nations against her, call together against her the kingdoms of Ararat, Minni, and Ashkenaz."

Tigranes was succeeded by Vahakin, who was celebrated for his personal strength, and was deified after his death. The dynasty came to an end with the next king, Vahi, who was defeated by Alexander the Great, B.C. 328.

The nation once more regained its freedom, B.C. 317, and raised Ardvates to the throne; but when he died, about thirty-three years later, the country fell into the hands of the Syrians. The Armenians were again in the hands of the Macedonians, when Antiochus the Great was overthrown by the Romans, about B.C. 190, and seized that opportunity for once more asserting their independence.

Some thirty or forty years later, the famous Parthian monarch, Mithridates I., placed his brother, Valarsaces, on the Armenian throne, and thus originated the great Arsacid dynasty, which lasted nearly six hundred years. This new ruler signalised his reign by founding cities, establishing just laws, rewarding virtuous citizens, and in every way promoting the prosperity of the nation.

His most famous successor was his great-grandson, Tigranes II., whose name was a glory to his people, as it was also a terror to his foes. He extended his territories from the Caspian Sea to the Mediterranean, and from the Caucasian Mountains to the Mesopotamian plains, including Syria, Cilicia, Assyria, Media, Atropatene, and Phœnicia. He would probably have become the founder of a mighty kingdom, had he not come into collision with the Romans. He ultimately submitted to Pompey, and was allowed to keep possession of his kingdom. At his death, about B.C. 55, he was succeeded by his son, Artavasdes, who assumed a more independent attitude, for which he was taken prisoner by Anthony, and transported to Egypt, where he was beheaded by Cleopatra, in the year B.C. 30.

During the next eighty years Armenia was in a state of practical anarchy. Although the country was nominally subject to the Roman power, no less than 170 native families managed to assert their own independence with more or less success. In the year A.D. 58, an usurper named Erovant succeeded in uniting the kingdom under his personal jurisdiction. He, in turn, was deposed by Ardashes, who was himself repeatedly dethroned and restored by the interference of the Parthian and Roman powers.

The next figure of prominence in the national history was Chosroes the Great, who took up arms in defence of the Arsacids, when they were driven from the Persian throne, and who was slain, in A.D. 232, by the Persian prince Anag, after which Armenia became subject to the Persians. All the royal family were murdered except Tiridates, a son of Chosroes, who contrived, in A.D. 259, to establish himself upon the throne, by the help of the Romans.

This reign will be for ever memorable for the establishment of Christianity in the land. For some time past the leaven had been working secretly, and St. Gregory the Illuminator was now busily engaged in the work of evangelisation. At first Tiridates persecuted the new religion, and threw the great evangelist into prison, but being healed of a dangerous disease through the good man's prayers, he himself embraced the Christian religion, and his example was followed by the majority of the people. The fire-temples were swept out of existence, and Christian churches and schools were established in every part of the land. Zoroastrianism received such a blow that all the machinations of its seven hundred magi were powerless to save it. Armenia became henceforward the bulwark of Christianity in Asia.

Needless to say, this meant for many years bitter opposition from the Persians—the great upholders of fire-worship—who not only resented the slight cast upon their national religion, but suspected that the Armenians would secure the powerful support of the Roman Empire. For a long period Armenia was the scene of continual struggles between these two great Powers, until finally the Roman emperor, Theodosius the Great, ceded the eastern part of the country to Persia, and annexed the western portion to the Roman Empire. Both Powers appointed representatives of the Armenian royal family to govern their respective provinces.

In the year A.D. 428 the last native ruler of Persian Armenia was deposed, and for two hundred years the country was governed by Persian officers, and the Christians were cruelly persecuted.

The sixth century saw a man arise who was to exercise an unique influence in Western Asia, and to shape the destinies of millions of human beings. The sandy plains of Arabia gave birth to Mohammed, that strange combination of prophet, warrior, and law-giver, under whose banner so much blood has been spilt and so many enormities committed by the fanatical hordes who have called themselves by his name. From A.D. 632 till 839

ABDUL HAMID II., SULTAN OF TURKEY.

Armenia was the theatre of incessant warfare between the Greeks and Mohammedans.

To adopt the language of a native writer: "Armenia has been over and over inundated with the blood of her inhabitants, enriched with their carcases scattered upon her face; her beautiful and bright sky was often rendered foggy and smoky on account of the conflagrations of her immense cities and numerous towns, kindled by the enemies; her beautiful sons and daughters were torn away from the bosoms of their parents, carried away as captives and sold for slaves; her magnificent churches and monasteries were converted into mosques and tekes. Yet the house of Togarmah marched on through all these tremendous seas of oppression, persecution, cruelty, and injustice, from a remote antiquity to the end of the fourteenth century of our era, lifting up the old—centuries old—flag of liberty, torn to pieces and ready to fall into an irreparable dissolution."

The close of the ninth century saw the downtrodden nation once more emerge into a position of practical independence. In A.D. 885, Ashcod I. ascended the throne and founded the dynasty of the Bagratidæ, who are supposed to be descended from King David. A period of prosperity ensued until A.D. 1079, when the Greeks seized a part of the country, and the Turks and Kurds made themselves masters of the rest. A few native princes maintained a precarious independence, and gradually a nominal kingdom was restored under the Rhupenian dynasty. This lasted till A.D. 1375, when the country was captured by the Saracens, and Leo IV., the last of the Armenian kings, was taken captive to Cairo. After serving a period of imprisonment, he was set at liberty, and ended his mortal career at Paris, on the 19th of November 1393.

Armenia never recovered from the blow. From

that day till now, her history has been one long chapter of oppression and cruel wrong. In the fourteenth century the Persians had possession of the north of Armenia, the Kurds of the south, and the Turks of the west. During the next century the land was mainly governed by the Persians. In 1604, Shah Abbas, in his contest with Sultan Ahmed I., devastated the whole country, and deported forty thousand of the inhabitants, who subsequently settled at Ispahan.

At length Russia approached, being welcomed by the Armenians as a deliverer from the tyranny of the Turks and Persians. The struggle continued from 1772 till 1827, when the Czar wrested from Persia the whole of the upper valley of the Araxes. At the conclusion of peace between Russia and Turkey, in 1829, the Russians retired from Erzeroum, which they had previously occupied, and great numbers of Armenians followed them, being afraid to fall into the hands of the Turks. By the Treaty of Berlin in 1878, Ardahan and Kars were ceded to Russia, together with 6687 square miles of Armenian territory. At the same time Great Britain guaranteed Turkey the integrity of her Asiatic possessions, on condition that she should thoroughly reform her administration and protect the Armenians from the ravages of the Kurds and Circassians. These promises the Sublime Porte has very characteristically ignored.

Thus it comes about that the northern portion of Armenia is in the possession of Russia, the south-eastern corner belongs to Persia, and the rest of the country still groans beneath the infamous misrule of Abdul Hamid II., "our Lord and Master the Sultan of the two Shores and the High King of the two Seas; the Crown of Ages and the Pride of all Countries, the greatest of all Khalifs; the Shadow of God on Earth; the successor of the Apostle of the Lord of the Universe; the Victorious Conqueror."

The Armenians, like the Jews, are now widely scattered. In addition to those living in their native land, there are communities at St. Petersburg, Moscow, and in South Russia. At Venice there is the well-known congregation of Armenian Mechitarists, and a great many representatives of the nation may be found in India. In London, Manchester, Amsterdam, and Marseilles are many Armenian merchants. In Manchester they are sufficiently numerous to support a native church. There are also a considerable number of Armenians in London, a great many refugees having arrived during the past few years. There are usually a few native students at Oxford and other British universities, and recently their number has considerably increased in America.

The total number of Armenians in the world has been variously estimated at from 2,500,000 to 4,000,000; but no exact figures are possible, as all statistics coming from Turkish official sources are open to the gravest suspicion.

CHAPTER III.

THE PEOPLE AND THEIR LANGUAGE.

THE Armenians are scientifically described as belonging to the Iranian group of the Indo-European family. They are, as a rule, of fine physique, being above middle stature, of darkish brown or yellow complexion, with black bushy hair, large nose, and wide rather than high forehead. Their expression is often slightly Jewish. The women are of graceful, erect carriage, with regular features and fine dark eyes.

The women cover their faces in the streets, and wear a long cloak similar to that of the Turkish women. The rest of their dress consists of loose, baggy trousers drawn in at the ankle, a coloured shawl fastened round the waist in three or four close folds, a linen shirt, and a short loose jacket. The head is swathed in a rag, and the hair is worn hanging down the back in five or six plaits. As for shoes, they seldom wear them.

The men wear similar loose, baggy cloth trousers tied at the ankle, a tight cotton waistcoat, over which is a coloured sack-like robe of cotton reaching below the knee and split up to the waist on either side. On their heads many of them wear the customary fez, with a dark cotton handkerchief tied round it; while on their feet are white woollen stockings and stout shoes.

The people dwell in towns and villages, clustering together for the sake of protection from Kurdish and Circassian robbers. The houses are usually of a sufficiently primitive character, being built mainly of undressed stone and sun-dried bricks. The roofs, which are supported by an arrangement of cross-beams and pillars, are covered with earth to a thickness of two or three feet. In those parts of Armenia where the winter is severe, the houses are usually more or less underground, and as the roofs and side-walls are not especially shapely the whole place often looks like an enormous rabbit-warren. A fall of snow makes it practically impossible to distinguish the dwellings from the refuse-heaps. The streets are narrow and irregular, and the sanitary arrangements are simply *nil*. Pavements are broken and rugged; the middle of the street forms an open sewer; refuse-heaps stand high in front of every habitation, and evil odours fill the air.

Some of the better-class houses form curious contrasts. The lower part resembles the dwelling of a humble workman, the irregular floors being simply trodden clay, and the staircase little better than a rough ladder, or sloping structure of rough stones. But upstairs will be found a large, well-furnished room, provided with sofas, easy-chairs, and a luxuriously cushioned divan in the window-space, affording a fine view of the neighbouring fields.

A country mansion in Armenia is a place to visit—once! When a man purposes to construct one of these abodes, he first clears a space of land, which in some cases will be nearly an acre in extent. Next he excavates the whole space to the depth of about five feet, setting apart a large area for the great cow-stable, which may be sixty or seventy feet each way. Some trees having been cut down, their trunks are roughly shaped into beams of eight or nine feet, the proposed height of the rooms, and are set up in rows, to serve as pillars to support the roof. The larger branches, without any shaping, are now laid across as beams, and the smaller branches and twigs arranged upon them, somewhat after the style of a thatched roof. A quantity of earth is next spread over all, and well trodden down; the turf, which formed the surface of the soil before it was disturbed, being finally laid upon the top. The whole structure then resembles a low, grass-covered mound.

The interior arrangements next receive attention. Living rooms are constructed round the stable, from which they are divided by rough stone walls plastered with clay or mud. These rooms are often numerous, and each has a stone fireplace opposite the door. The smoke is conducted up a chimney rising about two feet above the roof, and capped with a large flat stone to keep children and lambs from falling in. The smoke escapes through holes in the sides of the structure, which looks curiously like a large toadstool growing out of the grass-covered roof. There are stories of hungry thieves taking off the flat stone and fishing up the kettle, in which the food was stewing, with a hooked stick—not at all a difficult feat to perform.

The house is lighted by small projections in the roof or sides, resembling molehills, and carrying a small piece of glass or oiled paper. Each room is supplied with a simple iron lamp, and is rudely but comfortably furnished. On either side of the fireplace is a divan covered with Kurdish carpets, while a thick grey felt is laid upon the floor. Wooden pegs are inserted in the walls, and from these depend the garments and weapons of the inhabitants. Half-way up the chimney is a kind of damper, which can be opened and shut by means of a cord. In very cold weather it is usually shut, and the room becomes as hot and close as an oven.

The principal part of the house is devoted to the great cow-stable, which is often large enough to contain some dozens of cattle, which are kept here throughout the winter season, from October till about May. Their breath and heat warm the house; and when we mention that their litter is never removed, unless it becomes so thick that the animals are elevated dangerously near to the roof, the state of the atmosphere in an Armenian country house may be faintly imagined. In one corner of the great dark stable a wooden platform is raised about three feet from the floor, and railed round to keep the cows off. This is the reception room, and here the master of the house sits on a carpeted divan, and keeps an eye on the front door.

When spring arrives, the women and children come forth, red-eyed and blinking, into the unaccustomed air, and the half-melted snow is shovelled from the roofs. Great torrents of snow-water flow down the streets, and sometimes drown the little children. As soon as the ground is dry again, the fusty cattle are released from their eight months' captivity, and the work of clearing out the stable commences. This is a business of no small importance. Owing to the scarcity of wood, the principal fuel of the country is *tezek*, a compound of animal ordure and chopped straw. The litter of the stables is conveyed to the housetops, and for some days all the men and boys of the village are busy mixing and treading it to the required consistency, while the passing traveller devoutly wishes that he had been born without a nose.

After two or three days' drying, the *tezek* is cut into blocks and stored for use. When fresh, it gives off a thick, offensive odour; but when adequately dried, it burns without flame or smoke, and gives out a good heat. But it becomes very dusty when old, and the

European who attempts to move it finds that it has acquired properties analogous to those of the best Scotch snuff.

To change the subject, the bread of Armenia is almost as peculiar as the fuel. It is made in thin round cakes, about eighteen inches in diameter, flat like Scotch oatcake, but limp and flabby as a pancake. One of these is thrown on the table, like a damp napkin, in front of each guest. Occasionally it is used for the purpose of wrapping up other articles of food. The natives like to eat it folded round an onion or piece of cheese. It is baked by laying the dough on the bottom of a large cauldron, under which is a small fire. Another kind of bread is a hard-baked roll, several of which are usually hung together on a string. It is so very hard that it usually requires to be soaked in water before it can be eaten.

The following was the bill of fare at a banquet in honour of some English visitors:—

Cream with honey.
Soup.
Mutton chops and sliced potatoes.
Pastry saturated with melted sugar.
Fish cooked in oil.
Pastry with cheese in it.
Chopped meat and vegetables.
Rice-flour pastry.
Cucumbers stuffed with meat.
Roast chicken.
More chopped meat and vegetables.
Pilau.
Apples, pears, melons, grapes.

It sometimes happens in country places that the European guest finds even stranger viands set before him. A recent traveller relates the following adventure: "We dined à la Turc with our host and a friend, all pegging away out of the same dish with our fingers. We had Angora goat's flesh for dinner, as tough as indiarubber, and well it might be, as our

ARMENIAN PEASANT WOMEN WEAVING TURKISH CARPETS.

host explained that he never killed a goat until it was so old it would not breed, or because it was sick. We asked no questions, but hoped the one before us was only aged! Besides this, we had good soup, cucumber chopped up in bad vinegar, water-melons, and grapes. The air of the place must have been very hunger-producing, for, though we ate like wolves, we seemed never satisfied."

The villagers and country folk are mainly occupied with agricultural pursuits and cattle-breeding, their lands often being at a considerable distance from the village in which they live. Every morning and evening they may be seen going and returning, the unsettled state of the country not allowing them to live on their farms. Many of the families still live in patriarchal style, the younger sons and grandsons working with the hired servants on the land. Oxen and buffaloes are employed as beasts of draught, and the agricultural implements are of the most primitive kind.

In the large towns we find Armenians engaged in every kind of business. The goldsmiths, ironworkers, carpenters, masons, tailors, shoemakers, printers, dyers, weavers, and watchmakers of Asiatic Turkey are nearly all Armenians. Many also are bankers, brokers, physicians, and merchants. They have been called "The Anglo-Saxons of the East," and are noted both for their mechanical skill and for shrewd business tact. They strongly resemble their distant relatives the Jews, in commercial capacity and instinct for money-making.

The history of the nation proves that the Armenians were formerly a brave and warlike race, but long centuries of oppression have broken their spirit. Compelled to bow down before every passing Mussulman, and to give way to the rapacity of every avaricious Turk, they now go softly, in fear both of their goods and their lives, and seek by smooth speeches and obsequious bearing to avoid collision with their cruel persecutors. It is sad to witness the trembling humility with which an Armenian will bear himself in the presence of a Turk, and sadder still to see the eagerness with which the women and children hasten to hide themselves if an Ottoman soldier enters an Armenian house.

The language of the country belongs to the Iranian branch of the Indo-European family of languages. The old Armenian still survives in the native version of the Scriptures and in the public services of the Gregorian Church. It differs greatly from the spoken language of the present day, and in structure somewhat resembles classical Greek. The modern form is split up into three dialects, and contains a large admixture of Persian and Turkish words. There are thirty-eight letters in the native alphabet, which was amplified and developed by Miesrob in the fifth century. The order of writing is from left to right, contrary to the usual rule in Oriental languages.

The speech of the country sounds harsh and consonantal to a foreigner, the last syllables of the words being strongly accented. There is no inflection for gender—the words for *man* and *woman* being prefixed to indicate the sex of animals. The nouns have seven cases, and the verbs have four conjugations and four tenses.

The oldest existing fragments of pre-Christian Armenian literature are the cuneiform inscriptions at Van and a few ancient folk-songs. With the introduction of Christianity, literary activity greatly developed, though it mainly confined itself to the translation of works from the Greek and Syriac. Indeed, we are indebted to these translations for the preservation of certain important works which have perished in their original languages, such as the

Chronicle of Eusebius and some of the writings of Philo.

The fifth, twelfth, and thirteenth centuries were the greatest periods in Armenian literature, and in the eighteenth century another revival took place, the effects of which are still very apparent. The ancient writers have been re-edited, many new writers have come to the front, printing presses are established in nearly all Armenian towns, and periodical literature abounds. But the chief part of the literary productiveness of the nation is distinctly Christian in character.

CHAPTER IV.

THE CHURCH IN ARMENIA.

PROBABLY the earliest example of religious worship in Armenia must be connected with local traditions of the Deluge. When Noah and his family came out of the Ark, they are stated to have offered sacrifice to Jehovah, and for many years their descendants appear to have been pure monotheists. This is in accordance with the most ancient national traditions, which identify the country with the Ararat of the Bible.

The people, however, soon fell into idolatry, and the cuneiform inscriptions show us that their religion approximated very closely to that of Babylonia. Every tribe, city, and fortress appears to have possessed its own deity, but curiously enough there seems to have been no goddess in the system.

The influence of the Medo-Persian Empire at last made itself felt in the religion as well as in the political institutions of Armenia. Under its patronage, Zoroastrianism, or fire-worship, gradually drove out the grosser forms of idolatry, and for about nine centuries—from the end of the seventh century B.C. to the end of the third century A.D.—prevailed throughout the country.

The introduction of Christianity into Armenia has been supposed to date from the days of the apostles, or even of Christ Himself. A letter is still extant, said to have been written by Abgarus, king of Edessa and ruler of large part of Armenia, to our Lord, in which he refers to rumours of miracles, and invites Christ to visit Edessa, for the purpose of curing him of a disease. The answer purports to be written by the Apostle Thomas, and is to the effect that although Christ could not accept the invitation, He would send one of His disciples at a later date.

These two letters are recorded by the historian Eusebius, and were received as authentic by the early Church, but they are now rejected as forgeries by all scholars. It is also stated that the Apostle Thaddeus, accompanied by Bartholomew and Jude, first preached the gospel and established a Christian Church in Armenia about the year A.D. 34. Whether this tradition be true or false, it is pretty certain that there were Christians in the country as early as the first century of our era.

But the great evangelist of Armenia was St. Gregory the Illuminator. He was the son of Prince Anak, a member of the reigning family, and at the death of his father was carried away to Cæsarea in Cappadocia, where he received a Christian training. Returning towards the end of the third century, he commenced preaching the gospel, and for a reward suffered many a torture, and was imprisoned for thirteen years in a pit. At last his perseverance was rewarded by the conversion of King Tiridates and the recognition of Christianity as the national religion, and in A.D. 302 he was consecrated Bishop of Armenia. His successors assumed the title of Catholicos, and the national religious community is known as the Gregorian Church.

In A.D. 400 the Bible was translated into the language of the people by Bishop Miesrob and the Patriarch St. Isaac. Fifty years later the Persian king issued a decree forbidding all religions except

Zoroastrianism, and the Armenians, refusing to submit, suffered cruel persecutions. The spirit in which they met their foes has been well presented in a native song—

> "I will not be a heathen,
> I will not be a slave;
> If I cannot have a Christian's home,
> I'll find a Christian's grave."

In the year A.D. 451 the Council of Chalcedon was held, at which the Eutychian heresy, which taught that Christ did not possess both human and divine natures, was condemned. The bishops of Armenia were absent, owing to the Persian persecution, and forty years later the Armenian ecclesiastical authorities solemnly repudiated the decisions of the Council, and thus separated themselves from both the Eastern and Western Churches. They in this way secured a reputation for heterodoxy, which has clung to them ever since; but it would appear that the action of the Armenians arose rather from a misunderstanding than from any sympathy with the Eutychian error. Certainly at the present time the authoritative documents of the Gregorian Church are distinctly orthodox.

In their position of isolation, the Armenian bishops became more and more absorbed in home affairs, and kept the fire of patriotism alight in times of national distress. From time to time the Popes of Rome sought to persuade the Armenian Church to return to "the unity of the faith," and in the fifteenth century the Jesuit missionaries prevailed upon a large part of the Armenian Christians to unite with the Church of Rome. They are now known as the Catholic, or United Armenians, and have proved a great source of weakness to the original Gregorian Church. Much ill-feeling prevailed, and many petty persecutions took place, until the middle of the eighteenth century,

THE CHURCH IN ARMENIA 45

when the Catholicos sought the intervention of Peter the Great. Since that time Russia has been nominally the protector of the Armenian Church.

In doctrine the Gregorian Church is practically

ARMENIAN EX-PATRIARCH OF CONSTANTINOPLE.

identical with the orthodox Greek Church. It denies that the Holy Ghost proceeds from the Son as well as from the Father, and repudiates the Roman doctrines of purgatory, indulgences, and the supremacy of the Pope. At the same time, there is much to be desired. The public services are conducted, and the Bible is read, in the old Armenian tongue, which is not now understood by the common people, and something very much like the worship of saints and images is largely practised.

Seven sacraments are recognised both in the United and in the Gregorian Churches. In Baptism, the child is immersed three times, anointed with holy oil, confirmed, and permitted to receive the Communion. The Lord's Supper is administered in both elements to all Church members: the bread is unleavened, but the wine is not mixed with water. Confession must precede Communion, except in the case of very young children. Ordination is administered by anointing with holy oil, and only the priests receive extreme unction, which is administered immediately *after* death.

The liturgy is believed to date from the first century, and to have been an adaptation of that which was in use at Jerusalem. It is probably the oldest in the world, and was certainly used long before the time of Gregory the Illuminator, who considerably revised and enlarged it. Prayers are offered for the greater bliss of the pious dead, but the idea of purgatory is utterly repudiated.

The clergy include bishops, priests, and deacons, but the episcopal order is further subdivided into archbishops, bishops, and *vartabeds*, or doctors of theology. The clergy are also divided into black clergy, or monks, and white clergy, or parish priests. They may marry before ordination, but not afterwards. The priesthood is hereditary, the heir usually following some secular employment during his father's lifetime, and only receiving holy orders at his predecessor's death. None of the clergy are paid, but are wholly dependent upon the freewill offerings of the people. The archbishops, or patriarchs, are four in number, having their seats at Constantinople, Jerusalem, Sis, and Etchmiadzin.

For some years past, a Protestant reformation has been taking place in the country. In 1826 several Armenian clergymen at Beirut, in Syria, began travelling throughout Asia Minor preaching the gospel, and in 1831 the American Board of Foreign Missions first sent its agents to the Armenian community at Constantinople. The movement spread, and in 1843 a young convert was seized and beheaded in the streets of Constantinople, and his corpse was exposed for several days, as an insult to the Christians. The ambassadors of the great European Powers protested, and succeeded in extorting from the Sultan the following pledge :—

"The Sublime Porte engages to take effectual measures to prevent henceforward the execution and putting to death of the Christian who is an apostate."

Next came trouble from the authorities of the Gregorian Church. The Catholicos issued anathemas and excommunications in great profusion, and, as a consequence, the Protestants were stoned in the streets, unjustly imprisoned, ejected from their shops, invaded and plundered in their houses, bastinadoed, and abandoned by their friends. The result was only to give strength to the new movement. On the 1st of July 1846, the first Evangelical Armenian Church was constituted, and before the summer had ended three more were in existence.

In 1847 the Ottoman Government formally granted to the Protestant communities "all the rights and privileges belonging to others"; and at the close of the Crimean War the Sultan issued an edict in which he stated: "As all forms of religion are and shall be freely professed in my dominions, no subject of my empire shall be hindered in the exercise of the religion which he professes, nor shall he be in any way annoyed on this account." How much this promise was worth, subsequent events have abundantly shown.

The new movement rapidly grew, and in 1867 there were 56 churches, with 2000 communicants and 20,000 adherents. The most recent statistics we have been able to obtain stated that there were 110 churches and 11,095 members, 74 native ordained ministers and 129 preachers, and 85 other helpers, 203 places for stated preaching, 31,618 average attendants at the services, 21,655 Sunday-school children, and a Protestant community of 45,008 persons.

Since these figures were issued, many of the churches have been swept out of existence by the most relentless and barbarous persecution that the nineteenth century has witnessed.

CHAPTER V.

THE ORIGINS OF TROUBLE.

TO appreciate the causes of the long chapter of Armenian horrors which has culminated in the fearful atrocities of the past few years, we need to recall the incidents connected with the introduction of Christianity into the country. What the people are now suffering is neither more nor less than what they endured in the fifth and following centuries at the hands of the fire-worshipping Persians. If they had then returned to Zoroastrianism, or if, two centuries later, they had embraced Mohammedanism, when the soldiers of Islam massacred thousands of them in cold blood, the whole course of their subsequent history would have been changed.

It should never be forgotten that the question is essentially one of religion. The Turks have no reason for disliking the Armenians apart from this. Indeed, we venture to assert that they greatly prefer the industrious and peaceable Armenians to the idle and turbulent Kurds. But the Kurds are nominally Mohammedans, while the Armenians are very decided Christians. Hence the Kurds are allowed to have their way, and the Armenians are subjected to every indignity and outrage.

In the fourth century St. Chrysostom described the state of affairs in terms almost identical with those which have appeared in the columns of present-day newspapers.

"Like ferocious beasts they (the Kurds) fell upon the unhappy inhabitants of Armenia and devoured them. Trouble and disorder are everywhere. Hundreds of men, women, and children have been massacred; others have been frozen to death. The towns and villages are desolated; everywhere you see blood; everywhere you hear the groans of the dying, the shouts of the victors, and the sobs and the tears of the vanquished."

The *Times* has drawn attention to the fact that in the year 1360 some Armenian refugees were in England, seeking the protection of Edward III., and asking permission to make the woes of their country known. History is repeating itself to-day. The rule of the Turk during the past five hundred years has been productive of a never-ceasing stream of refugees, flowing towards happier shores.

Two hundred and fifty years ago, the English traveller, Sandys, published the following description of the sights he witnessed in Armenia:—

"The wild beasts of mankind have broken in upon them and rooted out all civility; and the pride of a stern and barbarous tyrant, possessing the thrones of ancient dominion, who aims only at the height of greatness and sensuality, hath reduced so great and goodly a part of the world to that lamentable distress and servitude under which it now faints and groans. Those rich lands at this present time remain waste and overgrown with bushes, and receptacles of wild beasts, of thieves and murderers; large territories dispeopled or thinly inhabited; goodly cities made desolate, sumptuous buildings become ruins, glorious temples either subverted or prostituted to impiety; true religion discountenanced and opposed; all nobility extinguished; no light of learning permitted, no virtue cherished; violence and rapine exulting over all, and leaving no security, save an abject mind and unlooked-on poverty."

In 1843 an incident occurred at Erzeroum, which is typical of the treatment habitually meted out to the Armenians by their Ottoman rulers. A merchant was sleeping at the caravanserai, with two soldiers near him. In the morning he found that his goods had been stolen, and charged the soldiers with the theft. They were taken before the judge, when they denied the charge, and were at once liberated. A Turkish woman now appeared, who had seen the soldiers burying the property at a certain place, where part of it was found after a little search. The soldiers were again arrested, and now stated that they had stolen half the property, and that an Armenian, named Artin, had taken the other half. This man was then arrested, but denied all knowledge of the affair, upon which the Pasha ordered him to be tortured till he should confess. A cord was tied round his head, two sheep's knucklebones were placed upon his temples, and the cord tightened till his eyes nearly came out. As he still declared his innocence, his teeth were drawn out one by one, pieces of cane were thrust under his toe nails and finger nails, and his thighs were torn with pincers. He was then hung up by the hands, and orders were given that he was to be tormented until he either confessed or died. This went on for twelve days before it came to the knowledge of the British Commissioners, who were then at Erzeroum, and who at once assumed an attitude which compelled the Pasha to release his victim.

It may be well here to briefly describe the old prison at Erzeroum, in which many a wretched Armenian disappeared for ever. It is now disused, though its modern substitute is bad enough.

In the floor of a dimly-lighted and ill-ventilated

cell, in the basement of the old clock tower, was a heavy wrought-iron grating, made of great bars some six inches apart, and strongly hinged and padlocked. When this grating was opened, there appeared under it the mouth of a narrow well cut in the rock, about two and a half feet in diameter, which sank down into the darkness far below. When the eye became accustomed to the gloom, a large white stone could be distinguished in the midst of the dungeon. This served as a table, and upon it the jailers threw down the prisoners' food. Sometimes they threw down a large piece of raw flesh as well, in order that its decomposition might add to the miseries of the wretched prisoners. The dungeon was bottle-shaped, between twenty and thirty feet deep, filth and vermin forming its only furniture. Into this awful hole many and many an innocent Armenian was let down, for no offence save that he was a Christian, and there he was left to perish unless his friends could provide a sufficiently large bribe to secure his release.

In the summer of 1877 occurred the Battak massacres, and in October of the same year a band of Turkish soldiers attacked a village near Yuzgat, and ordered the inhabitants to bring out all the money and food they possessed.

The terrified Armenians obeyed, and in a short time the whole band of soldiers were drunk. Then, in the words of the English Consul, "they made a hell of the place." The women, young and old, were outraged in the presence of their fathers, husbands, and brothers. All the cattle and horses were killed, and the village finally burnt to the ground. The scoundrels then departed for Yuzgat, forcing the men of the village to accompany them as porters, and in some cases actually riding on the men themselves. When the old and feeble broke down, they were forced to keep up by being pricked with knives and bayonets. Truly the horrors perpetrated by the slave-hunters of Africa are not worse than these!

On the night when the present Sultan of Turkey was proclaimed in the stead of his drunken, demented predecessor, a great wave of fanatical fury swept over the town of Beridjik, on the Euphrates. The cry was raised to kill the Armenians. All through the night bands of ruffians rushed through the streets, hammering at the doors of the Christians and threatening to murder them all. No one dared to have a light, and in the darkness whole families huddled together in the cellars, fearing even to speak. During that awful night children were prematurely born by mothers who died from fright, and many children lost their senses through sheer terror, and are babbling idiots to this day.

Without a doubt, the whole Christian population would have been murdered but for the strange apparition of an aged Turk in the streets, who was the sole survivor of the Deré Beys, and was regarded by the Moslems with peculiar veneration.

This man went everywhere demanding silence, and proclaiming that the peoples of the West were coming to avenge their fellow-Christians. He succeeded in stopping the riot; but, alas! his prophecy is still unfulfilled.

We have given the above instances to show that the persecution of the Armenians is neither a new thing nor a mere outbreak of spasmodic fanaticism. It has been the normal state of things in Asiatic Turkey for many years past. Other Powers have protested and threatened; the Sultan has again and again promised reforms; but the outrages have continued. Latterly it has become clear that the Ottoman Government has adopted a policy of extermination. The facts which have been published in Blue Books, and still more in the powerful articles of Canon MacColl and Dr. E. J. Dillon, have made this abundantly clear.

In 1892 the Sublime Porte issued decrees prohibiting Christian worship and education. This should be especially noted in view of the fact that by the Treaty of Berlin the same Government promised toleration for all religions, and the British Government received Cyprus as a pledge, and also as a recognition of the rights of England to see that the promise in question was duly carried out. How it has been carried out, we now proceed to show.

Christians are forbidden to build churches, and only after much delay and extensive bribes can they obtain permission to repair the old ones. There must be no bells, lest the religious feelings of the Mussulmans should be wounded, and for the same reason there must be no loud singing during the service. The most insulting language is applied to Christians in all public and official documents. They are described as "dogs" and "pigs," and in burial certificates they are said to be not "dead" but "damned." Here is a specimen:—

"We certify to the priest of the Church of Mary (in Armenia) that the impure, putrid, stinking carcase of ——, damned this day, may be concealed underground."

The above was not the spiteful work of a petty official: it was all quite in order, and was attested by the British Ambassador.

One of the Blue Books on "Religious Persecution in Turkey" states, on the authority of Her Majesty's Ambassador and Consuls, that the Porte has definitely refused to permit the establishment of Christian schools, and has prohibited the publication of the Bible in the Turkish tongue. In 1891 meetings for worship in private houses were forbidden. The next step was to prohibit Christian literature. So far did the authorities go in this direction, that even the classics of English literature, such as Shakespeare, Milton, and Scott, were confiscated. When Mr. Brooke Lambert, the Vicar of Greenwich, was travelling through Turkish territory in 1892, his pocket Bible was taken from him.

Christians are forbidden to quote passages of Scripture in their writings, lest revolutionary doctrines should be thus promulgated. Any passage from the Bible is prohibited which contains such words as persecution, courage, liberty, strength, king, arms, rights, etc. Even the word "star" is excluded, on the ground that the magi were led by a star to worship the Messiah, and this might encourage the Christians to look for a deliverer. Preachers are forbidden to inculcate the virtues of manly courage, resignation under affliction, and hope in God's delivering mercy. Such expressions as the following are strongly objected to:—

"The grace of God," because Mohammedans deny that Christians can have this grace; "good news or gospel," because it is not admitted that the teaching of Christ is good news; and "apostle," because Moslems deny that the first disciples of Christ were sent from God. On the other hand, books have been published containing the most abominable slanders about the Christian religion, and their authors have been decorated by the Sultan. It is not surprising, then, to learn that the work of Christian ministers and missionaries is beset by extraordinary difficulties.

In February 1893, Professor Thoumaian, of the Marsovan Protestant College, was arrested with several other Armenians on a charge of sedition, and for a time was treated with gross inhumanity, his hands being confined for five days in heavy manacles which cut into his flesh. He was also kept without food, and cruelly beaten. The charges against him were of the most absurd character. He had visited certain villages in connection with his mission work, and this was regarded as a cover for the spread of revolutionary teaching. No evidence whatever could be procured except the affidavits of some men who declared at the trial that they were tortured by the Government agents until they signed the documents. But notwithstanding these facts, M. Thoumaian and sixteen of his companions were sentenced to death, on the 12th of June, at Angora.

Happily for him, he was well known in England as a respected missionary and philanthropist. A great storm of indignation broke forth in all directions. Meetings to protest were held in many large towns, and urgent questions were asked in the House of Commons. Representations were at once made by the British Ambassador to the Porte, and he was informed that the case would be reconsidered by the Court of Cassation. But the British nation was in no mood to be trifled with. On 3rd July, Lord Rosebery sent the following telegram to Constantinople:—

"Her Majesty's Government cannot wait for result of proceedings of Court of Cassation. The Sultan is evidently determined to add to the cruel farce already perpetrated at Angora by another mock condemnation. Every additional day, however, that passes over the heads of these innocent prisoners is a new injustice."

The effect of this was instantaneous. On the following morning M. Thoumaian was set at liberty. It may be that other iniquities in Armenia would have been checked had the British Government held equally strong language on the subject.

Another step in the process of "diminishing" the Armenians was to reduce them to a condition of semi-starvation. The Ottoman Government is notori-

KURDISH MOUNTAINEERS OF SERDASHT.

ous for its unwillingness to pay its debts, and thus it comes about that the officials in charge of the various districts of Armenia have been left to live largely by their wits; in other words, by robbery and spoliation. Thus, Tahsin Pasha, a former Governor-General of Bitlis, made a practice of imprisoning scores of wealthy Armenians without the least pretext at a trial or even an accusation. Liberty was then offered in return for large money payments. Those prisoners who refused to pay the bribe were subjected to the most horrible tortures. Some were made to stand motionless for twenty-four, thirty-six, or forty-eight hours in a narrow box, bristling all over with iron spikes, and with hardly room on the ground to stand upon. About a hundred Armenians died in the prison of Bitlis alone.

In 1890, the village elder of Odandjor was a rich man, as wealth is reckoned in Armenia. He possessed eighty oxen, fifty buffaloes, six hundred sheep, several horses, and other property. He paid £50 a year in taxes to the Government. But he and his neighbours were plundered of their goods by the Turks, and in 1894 he was a homeless vagrant, in danger of dying from want.

In 1891 the Sultan began to form a force of thirty thousand Kurdish cavalry, officered by the most notorious brigands and criminals in Kurdistan. These men "openly state," wrote the British Consul at Erzeroum, "that they have been appointed to suppress the Armenians, and that they have received assurances that they will not be called to answer before the tribunals for any acts of oppression committed against Christians." These are the men who served as willing tools in the hands of the Sultan, whenever massacres and outrages were thought desirable.

The Kurds received general permission to feed their cattle in the pastures and cornfields of the

Armenians. Reuter's agent, who spent some months travelling about Armenia in disguise, states that wherever he went he found Kurdish cattle, with their attendants, in the pastures of the Armenians, who dared not resist or even complain.

The crops having been destroyed, a year's taxation was demanded in advance from the wretched Christians. When they pleaded poverty through the destruction of their crops, their cattle and household goods were promptly seized, and divided between the tax-gatherers and the Kurds. In this way thousands of Armenians have been reduced to feeding for months upon grass and roots, and hundreds have perished through sheer starvation. For a long time past, many of the people have been living upon coarse cakes, made of a mixture of roots, leaves, and grass, and looking very much like concrete.

The personal testimony of the gentleman alluded to was summed up in the following words: "I went to Armenia with my sympathies rather in favour of the Turks. I have come back with my blood boiling against their fiendish inhumanity. If the English people only realised the true state of the case, they would not endure it for a week."

The very scum of Turkish officialdom has been let loose upon the unhappy country. As an example we may mention Hussein Agha, whose doings have been thus described by Dr. E. J. Dillon, in the *Contemporary Review*:—

"Commanding a gang of Kurdish brigands, which could be increased to about two thousand men, he continually harassed the peaceful inhabitants of the province, plundering, torturing, violating, killing, till his name alone sent a thrill of terror to the hearts of all. The Armenians of Patnotz suffered so much from his depredations that they all quitted the village *en masse* and migrated to Karakilisse, where the

THE ORIGINS OF TROUBLE 61

Kaimakan resides; whereupon Hussein surrounded the house of the Bishop of Karakilisse with a large force, and compelled him to send the people back. Even the Mohammedans felt so shocked at his doings that the Mussulman priest of Patnotz, Sheikh Nari, complained of him to the Governor-General of Erzeroum. Hussein then sent his men, who murdered Sheikh Nari and frightened his daughter-in-law to death. In one expedition he carried off 2600 sheep, many horses, kine, etc., took £500, burnt nine villages, killed ten men, and cut off the right hands, noses, and ears of eleven others. Early in the year 1890 he outraged five Christian girls of Patnotz, and in September and October of the same year he levied a contribution of £300 on the people of the same district. *For none of these crimes was he ever tried.* In December 1890 he sent his brother to raise more money, which was done by raiding twenty-one villages of the Aintab district, the net result being £350 and 3000 lbs. of butter. Hatsho, an Armenian of Patnotz, who could not, or would not, contribute a certain sum to his coffer, had his house raided in his absence, and his wife and two children killed. All this time the gallant Hussein occupied the post and discharged the duties of a Mudir, or Deputy Sub-Governor. One day he drove off one thousand sheep and seven yoke of buffaloes from Patnotz and Kizilkoh, and sold them in Erzeroum to a merchant, after which he confiscated a fine horse belonging to Manook, an Armenian of Kizilkoh, and sent it as a present to the son of an Erzeroum judge. One night, towards the end of February 1891, Hussein and others entered the house of an Armenian, Kaspar, for the purpose of carrying off Kaspar's handsome daughter-in-law. The inmates, however, shouted for help, whereupon Hussein, raising his revolver, shot the young woman dead. A petition was presented asking that he might be punished, but the Vali of Erzeroum declined to receive it, and Hussein was summoned to Constantinople, welcomed with cordiality, decorated by His Majesty, raised to the rank of Pasha, and appointed Brigadier-General."

It is the fashion with the Sultan and his ministers to declare that all instances of oppression and outrage are the work of disorderly local officers, and are neither sanctioned nor approved by the authorities at Constantinople. But is it possible for any sane person to believe these protestations in view of the fact that the perpetrators of outrages not only escape punishment, but have been repeatedly promoted and decorated at the hands of the Sultan himself?

The case we have just quoted is not exceptional, but strictly typical. Everywhere throughout Turkish Armenia the same misrule prevails, and the same policy of extermination is rigorously pursued. Whole provinces have been decimated, and some—Alaschkerd, for instance—almost entirely cleared of Armenians. "Over twenty thousand woe-stricken wretches, once healthy and well-to-do," says Dr. Dillon, "fled to Russia or to Persia, in rags and misery, deformed, diseased, or dying; on the way they were seized over and over again by the soldiers of the Sultan, who deprived them of the little money they possessed, nay, of the clothes they were wearing; outraged the women in the presence of their sons and daughters, and then drove them over the frontier to hunger and death. The Christians, by whose toil and thrift the empire was held together, were despoiled, beggared, chained, beaten and banished, or butchered. First their movable wealth was seized, then their landed property was confiscated, next the absolute necessaries of life were wrested from them, and finally, honour, liberty, and life were taken with as little ado as if these Christian men and women were wasps or mosquitoes. Thousands of Armenians were thrown into prison, and tortured and terrorised till they delivered up the savings of a lifetime, and the support of their helpless families, to ruffianly parasites. Whole villages were attacked in broad daylight by the Imperial Kurdish cavalry, without pretext or warning, the male inhabitants turned adrift or killed, and their wives and daughters transformed into instruments to glut the foul lusts of these bestial murderers. During the year 1894, in the districts of Boolanyk and Moush alone, upwards of ten thousand head of cattle and sheep were driven off by the Kurds.

This was the method in vogue all over the country; the details varied according to the condition of things, places, and kinglets, but the means and ends never varied. The result is the utter disappearance of wealth, and the rapid spread of misery, so intense, so irremediable, so utterly loathsome in its moral and physical effects as to have inspired some of its victims with that wild courage akin to madness, which always takes its rise in despair. This has been the *normal* condition of Armenia ever since the Treaty of Berlin."

CHAPTER VI.

THE SASSOUN MASSACRE AND THE COMMISSION OF INQUIRY.

"I SEEK refuge with Allah from Satan the accursed. In the name of Allah the Compassionate, the Merciful! O Lord of all creatures! O Allah! Destroy the infidels and polytheists, thine enemies; the enemies of the religion! O Allah! Make their children orphans, and defile their abodes! Cause their feet to slip; give them and their families, their households and their women, their children and their relations by marriage, their brothers and their friends, their possessions and their race, their wealth and their lands, as booty to the Moslems, O Lord of all creatures!"

The above pretty sample of cursing is a literal translation of the official prayer of Mohammedanism, which is used daily throughout the Turkish Empire. It should be noted that Christians are included amongst the "infidels" referred to in the prayer. How the Turks have endeavoured to fulfil their own petition has been shown in the previous chapter, and will now appear in even more lurid colours.

We have seen how, ever since the Treaty of Berlin, the Ottoman Government had been taking steps to finally settle the Armenian question by the simple expedient of exterminating the nation. They had reduced the milder and less spirited inhabitants of the plains by extortion, robbery, and imprisonment; now they began to turn their attention to the hardier and braver tribes dwelling in the mountainous districts of the Bitlis vilayet. It is practically impossible to arrive at exact facts, but it appears certain that secret orders were issued to exterminate the Christians of Sassoun. Rumours to this effect were abroad for many months, and a long report was sent by the Abbot of Moush to the British agent at Erzeroum, informing him of the plan, and appealing for aid from the English people. Nothing, however, was done, and in the autumn of 1894 the fearful massacre took place which has shocked the conscience of the entire civilised world.

In May 1893 an agitator named Damatian was captured near Moush, and this was made a pretext for massing the Kurdish irregular cavalry in the district. During June the people of Talvoreeg saw the Kurds gathering day by day, to the number of several thousands, and began to make preparations to defend themselves. On the eighth day a battle took place, and the villagers succeeded in holding their own, about a hundred of the Kurds being slain. Upon this, the Governor-General of Moush announced that the Armenians were in revolt, and set out with troops and two field-pieces. He did not, however, attack the village, but contented himself with besieging it. This state of things was ended by the breaking up of summer, and all through the terrible winter the villagers were left alone.

In the early spring, it appears that the Kurds were encouraged to attack the various villages of the Sassoun district, while troops were sent from Moush and Bitlis to restore "order." It is a significant fact that they took with them ten mule-loads of kerosene. Then the villages were again besieged, the inhabitants occasionally making sorties to obtain food. "The Kurds on one occasion stole several oxen, and their owners tracked their property to the Kurdish tents, and found that one ox had been butchered. They asked for the others, and were refused, whereupon the villagers left, and later returned with some companions. A scrimmage ensued, in which two or three were killed on either side. The Kurds promptly took their dead to the Government at Moush, and reported that the region was filled with Armenian and foreign soldiers. The Government at once sent in all directions for troops, gathering in all from eight to ten regiments, and the Kurds congregated to the number of about twenty thousand, while some five hundred of the irregular Kurdish cavalry were brought to Moush.

"At first the Kurds were set on, and the troops kept out of sight. The villagers, put to the fight, and thinking they had only the Kurds to do with, repulsed them on several occasions. The Kurds were unwilling to do more unless the troops assisted. Some of the troops then assumed Kurdish dress, and helped them in the fight with more success. Small companies of the troops next entered several villages, saying they had come to protect them as loyal subjects, and were quartered among the houses. *In the night they arose and slew the sleeping villagers, man, woman, and child.* By this time those in the other villages were beginning to feel that extermination was the object of the Government, and desperately determined to sell their lives as dearly as possible. Then began a campaign of butchery that lasted some twenty-three days, or, roughly, from the middle of August to the middle of September."[1]

The above quotation from the testimony of an American citizen at that time resident in Armenia, affords a significant comment upon the official explanation of the Ottoman Government that the

---

[1] From Rev. F. D. Greene's *Armenian Crisis*, by kind permission of Messrs Hodder & Stoughton.

Armenians were in a state of insurrection, and that the outrages were the work of the nomad Kurdish tribes. Notwithstanding the utter—and obviously intentional—failure of the Commission of Inquiry to clear up the facts, it is evident from the testimony of Armenian Christians, of native clergy, of Protestant missionaries, of British consuls, and of special commissioners who visited the district, that the massacres at Sassoun were the work of Turkish soldiers, both regular and irregular, and were executed under the direct orders of Ottoman officials. When it is remembered that the Sultan shortly afterwards decorated Zekki Pasha, who led the troops in the work of extermination, and also sent silken banners by special messenger to the four leading Kurdish chiefs, it is impossible for any man in his senses to believe that the Armenian atrocities were either disapproved or regretted by the Government at Constantinople.

The first intimation that something was wrong reached the British Government on 31st August, at which time the massacre was at its height. Sir Philip Currie, Her Majesty's Ambassador to the Porte, telegraphed as follows: "I have been informed at the Porte, in answer to an inquiry, that Armenians at Talori, in the vilayet of Bitlis, have risen, and that in order to quell the revolt a small number of troops are being sent to the scene." Again, on the 4th of September: "I have questioned the Grand Vizier on the subject, and he stated that the Armenians had risen, and that considerable bloodshed had taken place." Rumours soon began to spread that shocking barbarities had been committed, and Vice-Consul Hallward was instructed to proceed at once to the scene. The Turkish officials then endeavoured to seclude the district from all outside intercourse by a report of cholera, and actually prevented the British representative from visiting Sassoun. He, however, succeeded in ascertaining the general facts, as will appear from the following extract from his report, dated Moush, October 9, 1894:—

"Last year the Vali of Bitlis summoned some of the chief men from these villages on some pretext to Bitlis, but they did not appear, His Excellency Hassan Tahsin Pasha being notorious for his skill in exploiting 'the Armenian question.' There is, I believe, scarcely a single well-to-do Armenian in Bitlis or Moush who has not been either imprisoned or threatened with imprisonment on charges of sedition with a view to the extortion of money. The individuals in question, fearing similar treatment, preferred to remain at home. This appears to have exasperated His Excellency, and, taking advantage of certain disturbances that occurred last year between the Kurds and Armenians, he in the middle of June last sent a battalion of soldiers to that district, nominally to protect the Armenians. At the same time, a certain Kurdish sheikh, Mehemet by name, was brought to Moush from the Diarbekir region, and commissioned to collect large numbers of tribal Kurds, who accordingly assembled in July last in great numbers in the Talori district.

"Meantime the battalion of soldiers had lived on peaceable terms with the villagers for some six weeks, when, about the beginning of August, some Bekiranli Kurds from Diarbekir stole some cattle from one of the villages, and on the Armenians attempting to recover them a slight affray ensued, in which two or three were killed and wounded on either side. Thereupon the Kurds came to Moush to complain to the Government, saying that all the Armenians were up in arms, and that there were foreigners among them instigating them to revolt. The commander of the troops is said to have reported to the same effect.

"The Vali then demanded large reinforcements of troops, which were accordingly sent from Erzinjian, Kharput, Diarbekir, Erzeroum, and Van. When they appeared on the scene, the Armenians surrendered to them on promise of protection against the Kurds. The troops then proceeded to massacre those who had surrendered, and everybody else they could lay hands on—men, women, and children. They plundered all the property they could carry off, and then burnt the houses. The work of massacre and pillage is said to have continued for several days, and some twenty-five villages were almost entirely destroyed. The Kurds drove off enormous quantities of sheep and cattle, *but did not assist in the massacre to any great extent.* They are said to have carried off a number of girls, and many others were raped by the soldiers. Churches were sacked and burnt, and priests' robes and church ornaments were publicly sold in the market of Moush. I have heard that shocking atrocities were committed, such as burying men alive, blowing them up with gunpowder, etc. A woman from Talori told me that thirty men had been buried alive by soldiers, and I have heard the same thing repeated in different quarters, but I am not in a position to sift the truth of such stories.

"Nor is it possible for me to estimate the loss of life, but from all I have heard I suppose there must have been a thousand or more killed. I saw one old man who had been wandering for about three weeks in the mountains with a small boy, and had at length taken refuge in a monastery. He was from the village of Ghelieguzan, and was a rich man, there being forty persons in his house. He did not know for certain what had become of any of them except the boy, but he supposed most of them must have been killed. In another case I heard of, six escaped out of a household of fifty. There are a few women and children in a destitute state in the town, and a few in some of the villages in the plain, and some have taken refuge with the Kurds of Sassoun.

Others are wandering about the mountains, as the Armenians about here are afraid to receive them in their houses. . . .

"Had it not been for the attitude of the authorities in refusing to allow me to visit the district, and preventing me as far as possible from having any communication with the population here or elsewhere, by putting police to watch this house and to follow me wherever I go, I might have supposed there was some exaggeration in the accounts I have heard. But their object, evidently, is to stave off any close inquiry into the matter till winter, when all the mountainous districts will be under snow, and communication with the outside world extremely difficult: by the spring they, no doubt, calculate the whole affair will have blown over."

The same gentleman, writing on 6th November, was able to give the following additional particulars:—

"The General, who came from Erzinjian, read an Imperial Firman, authorising the punishment of the villagers, and exhorted the soldiers not to fail in their duty. It is said that at first they hung back, not relishing their task, but their officers urged them on with threats, and the work of destruction and butchery was carried through without mercy or distinction of age or sex.

"A large number of the leading men, headed by a priest, went out to meet the commanding officer with their tax receipts in their hands, by way of proving their loyalty to the Government, and begging for mercy. They were surrounded and killed to a man.

"At Ghelieguzan a number of young men were bound hand and foot, laid out in a row, had brushwood piled on them, and were burnt alive.

"At another village a priest and several leading men were captured and promised release if they would tell where others had fled to; they did so, but were killed. The priest had a chain put round his neck and pulled in opposite directions, so that he was nearly throttled; finally, bayonets were placed upright in the ground, and he was tossed in the air so that he fell on them.

"The men of another village fled with their women and children to a grotto, where they remained for several days, till the weaker ones died of hunger; the remainder were at last discovered by the soldiers and put to the bayonet, which was the weapon principally employed throughout.

"Some sixty young women and girls were driven into a church, where the soldiers were ordered to do as they liked with them, and afterwards kill them, which order was carried out.

"A larger number of the most attractive women were set aside and invited to accept Islam and marry Turks; they refused, and were accordingly killed.

"The petroleum brought from Bitlis was utilised for burning the houses, together with the inhabitants inside them. A soldier related in Bitlis how he had seen on one occasion a little boy run out from the flames, and pushed back into them with a bayonet by another soldier. It was also used to burn the corpses.

"Many other disgusting barbarities are said to have been committed, such as ripping open pregnant women, tearing children to pieces by main force, etc.: but the above will serve as examples of the way in which this campaign of extermination was carried out. . . .

"The final scene was enacted in the valley of Talvoreeg, where a large number of men, women, and children had collected; they were surrounded by Kurds and soldiers, and first thinned out by rifle-shots, and then the rest despatched with sword and bayonet. The operations lasted some twenty-three days, from about the 18th of August to the 10th of September, having been begun by the Bitlis and Moush garrisons, who were gradually reinforced by other troops of the 4th Army Corps. . . .

"The details given above were principally collected from soldiers who took part in the massacre, and I have heard the main facts substantiated from various different quarters, among others by a Turkish zaptieh, who was there and saw the whole affair."

These terrible statements are not the exaggerations of Armenian agitators, or the wild rumours of fanatical and ill-informed partisans; they are the official report of the British representative on the spot, after careful and discriminating inquiry in many directions. At the risk of horrifying the reader, we must add a few further details, gathered in the neighbourhood by American citizens and missionaries, who took them down from the lips of reliable eyewitnesses, and published both in England and in the United States by the Rev. F. D. Greene, M.A., who was for many years a resident in Armenia:—

"Children were placed in a row, one behind another, and a bullet fired down the line, apparently to see how many could be despatched with one bullet. Infants and small children were piled one on the other and their heads struck off."

"A large and strong man, the chief of one village, was captured by the Kurds, who tied him, threw him on the ground, and, squatting around him, stabbed him to pieces."

"Children were frequently held up by the hair and cut in two, or had their jaws torn apart. Women with child were cut open; older children were pulled apart by their legs. A handsome, newly-wedded couple fled to a hilltop: soldiers followed, and told them they were pretty, and would be spared if they would accept Islam, but the thought of the horrible death they knew would follow did not prevent them from confessing Christ."

ARMENIAN MOUNTAINEER OF SHADOKH.

"Many of the dead were thrown into trenches, which the rain had washed out, and were covered with earth. Where no such trenches existed, the bodies were piled up with alternate layers of wood, saturated with kerosene, and set on fire."

"In one place, the women, after being forced to serve the vile purposes of a merciless soldiery, were taken to a valley near by and hacked to pieces with sword and bayonet."

"To some of the more attractive women in one place, the proposition was made that they might be spared if they denied their faith. 'Why should we deny Christ?' they said, and pointing to the dead bodies of their husbands and brothers before them, they nobly answered, 'We are no better than they; kill us too,'—and they died."

"The soldiers talk quite freely about matters at Sassoun. There was great spoil,—flocks, herds, household goods, etc.,—but their chief work was to dispose of the heaps and heaps of the dead. The stench was awful. They were gathered into the still standing houses and burned with the houses."

"I saw an eyewitness to some of the Sassoun destruction. He passed through three villages. They were all in ruins, and mutilated bodies told the horrible tale. For four or five days he was in one village. During the day parties of the scattered inhabitants would come in and throw themselves upon the mercy of the officer in command. About two hours after sundown each evening, these prisoners of that day were marched out of camp to a neighbouring valley, and the air was rent with their pitiful cries. He saw nothing more of them."[1]

The following additional particulars from Armenian sources have appeared in the London press:—

"The Kurds killed people with bullets and daggers,

[1] Rev. F. D. Greene's *Armenian Crisis*.

but the soldiers delighted in torture. They put some to death with scissors, cutting them and opening veins in the neck. Others were sawed, others had their tongues cut out, eyes gouged out, and several fingers removed before death. I saw men and women thus mutilated, and they lay about the camp for two hours before they died."

"I saw a Turkish sergeant bind an old Armenian, head downwards, to two or three branches, and slowly cut him through with an axe. From this hiding-place I saw soldiers torturing Priest Ohannes of Semal, and Priest Der Arakel. Their eyes were gouged out, and they uttered horrible cries, and implored the soldiers to put them out of pain. But the soldiers made them dance, and for some time they danced, screaming with pain. Then the soldiers bayoneted them. When the dead were examined, the body of Priest Ohannes, whose corpse had still a rope round the neck, was identified. The eyes had been gouged out, and nose, ears, and lips cut off, and the skin flayed from both sides of the head."

"Just fancy such a picture as this, which actually occurred at Sassoun:—'I bet you ten *tshireks* I'll cut clean through the necks of four Christian puppies at one stroke of my *khama*!' exclaimed one Turkish soldier. 'Done!' cry half a dozen of his comrades. And the trial is made at once. Four Christian children are pulled out of their mother's arms amid heartrending screams and piteous prayers, and are then tied one on top of the other, head upon head, neck upon neck. Then the man who made the bet approaches with his sharp scimitar, touches the neck of the topmost just to measure his stroke, raises his trusty steel, and, with a swift sweep and a deft backward movement, produces a rivulet of blood, which runs along between the quivering little trunks and the bloody heads which have rolled on to the thirsty earth."

Amid all these horrors one deed of woman's heroism called forth the admiration of the world. It has thus been described:—

"The women of one village defended their position for twenty-four hours against the besiegers, but finally yielded to greater numbers. They scarcely left their camp when they found that they were surrounded on all sides. Their condition was terrible; many carried their babies on their backs, while the elder children stood by their mothers in the fight. They soon saw that they could never fight their way through the ranks of the enemy. Then the wife of Grgo stepped on a rock and cried, 'My sisters, you must choose between two things. Either fall into the hands of these Turks, and forget your husbands, your homes, your holy religion, and adopt the Mohammedan faith, and be dishonoured, or you must follow my example.' With these words, holding her year-old baby in her arms, she dashed herself from the rock into the abyss. She was followed by a second, a third, a fourth woman. Without a sound, one body fell after another. The unhappy children followed like lambs the example of their mothers. Very soon the ravine was strewn with corpses. . . . The heroine who first cast herself from the rock was called Schakhe, and her name deserves to be known throughout Europe."

Surely we have told enough. The very pages seem to drip with blood, and yet we have not told all. There are other incidents within our knowledge so awful that we cannot bring ourselves to write them down. What we have here recorded is surely enough to make the blood boil in the veins and the tears flow from the eyes of even the most callous reader.

When information of the Sassoun massacre reached the British Ambassador at Constantinople, he at once made formal representations to the Sultan, who promptly contradicted the reports, and charged Vice-Consul Hallward with instigating the Armenians to revolt. This charge was duly reported to the British Government, and Colonel Chernside was ordered to proceed at once to Sassoun and investigate the whole affair. But investigation by an impartial authority was precisely what the Porte most feared, and after considerable manœuvring to defeat the intentions of England, the following message was delivered to Sir Philip Currie on the 15th of November:—

"His Imperial Majesty will send before to-morrow week a Commission to inquire into the events which have taken place in the Sassoun district, as well as into all the reports mentioned in the Memorandum presented to His Imperial Majesty by Her Majesty's Embassy on the 1st November.

"The Sultan considers that it is in his own interest to inquire into the facts as reported, and assures Her Majesty's Ambassador that the inquiry will be carried out in a just and impartial manner, and that punishment will fall on the guilty. The Commission will be composed of two or three Imperial aides-de-camp and of a civil functionary, all trustworthy men, who will be sworn to give a true report. His Majesty does not believe in the charges which have been brought against Vice-Consul Hallward of inciting the Armenians to rebellion; he considers them null and void, and withdraws them."

No sooner had this proposal been accepted by the British Government than the wiles of the Turk became apparent. An official notice was sent to the papers, announcing that there had been no outrages, and that the Commission was only sent to inquire into the criminal conduct of Armenian brigands. This policy was pursued until the patience of England was exhausted, and on 30th November the Cabinet sent the following intimation to the Sultan:—

"In these circumstances, Her Majesty's Government feel it their duty to protest formally against an inquiry so entirely unsatisfactory, as insufficient to fulfil the engagements entered into by the Sublime Porte under the 61st Article of the Treaty of Berlin, and in presence of the grave situation thus created they must reserve to themselves entire liberty of action in regard to the whole matter."

The veiled threat thus conveyed had the result of securing promises from the Porte that the Armenian outrages should be investigated, and it was arranged that Consular representatives of England, France, and Russia should be present at the sittings of the Commission. But it must be distinctly understood that they formed no part of the Commission, and had no power to examine witnesses, except through the Turkish officials who conducted the inquiry.

The Commission held its first meeting at Moush on the 24th of January 1895, and completed its inquiry on the 1st of June. The whole business proved to be a complete farce; the selection of witnesses was left in the hands of local Turkish officials, and the Commissioners exhibited most discreditable bias in their proceedings. Only with the greatest difficulty could the Consular Delegates obtain permission to examine Armenian witnesses, and when this was done, the officials promptly brought forward a mass of rebutting evidence. Most of the Armenians examined were plainly in a state of extreme terror, and refused to give evidence, while some admitted that they had been tortured as a foretaste of what they would receive if they told the truth. Nothing is more manifest, from a careful reading of the *procès-verbaux*, than that the inquiry was altogether one-sided and inadequate. The most absurd and contradictory evidence was accepted on the Turkish side, while evidence on the other side was promptly discredited. As a specimen of the methods by which witnesses were prepared for the Commission, the following quotation from a letter from the Vice-Consul at Van is significant:—

"A Sassoun prisoner was so beaten on his way here that he died soon after. Two others have since died. They had been repeatedly beaten, half starved, and, in this cold weather and in these damp dungeons, had on only a coarse, ragged cotton shirt and drawers. Inquisitional methods are being used to get these prisoners to testify that the leading Armenians here now in prison have been in league with them. Now that the Commission is afoot, they want them to testify that the Government had nothing to do with destroying villages, but merely stepped in to restore order between them and the Kurds."

On 29th April the three Consular Delegates telegraphed to their Ambassadors as follows:—

"Hebo, of Shenik, was summoned by us to-day, and deposed that the Chief of Gendarmerie yesterday threatened him with death if he accused the soldiers instead of the Kurds of killing the Armenians; that by means of Nadir Agha and the Mufti acting as interpreters, he received a similar recommendation from the Mutessarif in the presence of a Pasha, *and of the Secretary of the Commission.*

"Further promises were made by the Mutessarif that he would give him 1000 piastres, 10 oxen, and 500 sheep, reconstruct his house and his village, making him Headman of the latter, and restore the £T. 360 taken from his brother, on condition that he would acknowledge that he had seen Mourad, whose revolutionary counsels had been followed by the Armenians; that he would attribute the burning of the villages to the Kurds, declare that Mourad and his band had fought with the troops at Ghelieguzan; and, finally, that he would refuse to reply when questioned about the massacre of the women in the church, or about the priest of Semal."

Without any investigation, the Commission declared this statement to be false, on the bare denial of some of the persons accused. What possible value can attach to an Inquiry conducted on such principles?

On 8th May the Commissioners were at Ghelieguzan, and, after much objection, allowed the Consular Delegates to open some of the trenches. We give the result in the words of the official report:—

"Two of these trenches were opened in their presence. In the first they found only fragments of clothing. Round the second, a space of some thirty yards by ten was strewn with pieces of human bones and bits of clothing; amongst other things they saw two skulls, and in the trench they found, among fragments of bone and clothing, a putrefied corpse clothed, and three skulls, one of which had still some hair adhering to it, and contained a portion of the brain. The peasants, however, refused to continue the digging on account of the nauseating smells.... They, however, made the villagers dig up a fourth place near the village, and this brought to light a decapitated trunk, an arm with its hand, three skulls, and some small bones. The smells here were again overpowering. The villagers stated that on their return they had themselves removed many bodies from the three trenches, and buried them near the church.

"The Delegates found the village itself, which had contained something like one hundred and twenty houses, entirely burnt out, and the thirty families still left living in a destitute condition in huts.... The Delegates left on the 9th of May, and for the first three hours Mr. Shipley reports that their line of march was dotted with hamlets of from five to twenty houses completely ruined, not even the walls being left standing."

It is needless to say that when the official report of the Commission was issued, it proved to be utterly inconclusive and worthless. Many trivial matters had been threshed out at wearisome length, but the main charges, to investigate which the Commission was professedly appointed, had been in every case practically ignored. How the British representative, Mr. Shipley, was impressed by it, may best be gathered from an extract from his report:—

"I do not think, seeing as I did, in company with my colleagues, the entire ruin of a whole district, not a house being left standing, the fields even having been wantonly devastated, as well as the abject misery and destitution to which these Armenians have been reduced, that the epithets applied to the conduct of the Turkish soldiers and Kurds by the press are in any way too strong. We have in our Report given it as our conviction, arrived at from the evidence brought before us, that the Armenians were massacred without distinction of age or sex; and, indeed, for a period of some three weeks, it is not too much to say that the Armenians were absolutely hunted like wild beasts, being killed wherever they were met, and if the slaughter was not greater it was, I believe, solely owing to the vastness of the mountain ranges of that district, which enabled the people to scatter, and so facilitated their escape. In fact, and speaking with a full sense of responsibility, I am compelled to say that the conviction has forced itself on me that it was not so much the capture of the agitator Monrad, or the suppression of a pseudo-revolt, which was desired by the Turkish authorities, as the *extermination, pure and simple*, of the Ghelieguzan and Talori districts."

CHAPTER VII.

THE WORK OF EXTERMINATION.

A FEW months ago, three hundred and six of the chief men of Khnouss addressed a petition to "the humane and noble people of England." In it they say:—

"We now solemnly assure you that the butchery of Sassoun is but a drop in the ocean of Armenian blood shed gradually and silently all over the empire since the late Turko-Russian War. Year by year, month by month, day by day, innocent men, women, and children have been shot down, stabbed, or clubbed to death in their houses and their fields, tortured in strange, fiendish ways in fetid prison cells, or left to rot in exile under the scorching sun of Arabia. During the progress of that long and horrible tragedy no voice was raised for mercy, no hand extended to help us. That process is still going on, but it has already entered upon its final phases, and the Armenian people are at the last gasp. Is European sympathy destined to take the form of a cross upon our graves?"

Apparently the Sultan of Turkey answered this question in the affirmative,—not altogether without reason,—and last autumn (1895) his agents set massacres on foot throughout all the Armenian districts.

On 30th October occurred a fearful massacre at Erzeroum. Without any apparent cause, the Turkish soldiers suddenly appeared in the streets and deliberately shot down every Armenian Christian they could see. Rushing through the streets, they fired into the native houses, and then proceeded to loot the goods. The American Mission buildings and the British Consulate were for the next few days crowded to suffocation with trembling Armenian women and weeping children, lamenting their missing husbands and brothers, and fearing that every hour would prove their last. Those who had failed to escape from their houses before the looting commenced, were savagely murdered by the soldiers. In one house two young brides were found lying on carpets bespattered with blood, disfigured and almost naked. In another house were two men butchered in a barbarous way, splinters of broken boxes and doors, windows shattered to pieces, the plastering torn and broken, everything in ruin.

"What I myself saw this Friday afternoon," wrote the *Times* correspondent, "is for ever graven on my mind as the most horrible sight a man can see. I went to the Armenian Gregorian cemetery. The municipality had sent down a number of bodies, friends had brought more, and a horrible sight met my eyes. Along the wall on the north, in a row 20 feet wide and 150 feet long, lay three hundred and twenty-one dead bodies of the massacred Armenians. Many were fearfully mangled and mutilated. I saw one with his face completely smashed in with a blow of some heavy weapon after he was killed. I saw some with their necks almost severed by a sword cut. One I saw whose whole flesh had been skinned, his fore-arms were cut off, while the upper arm was stripped of flesh. I asked if the dogs had done this. 'No, the Turks did it with their knives.' A dozen bodies were half burned. Many of the corpses had been rifled of all their clothes except a cotton under-garment or two. These white under-clothes were

A GRIM CORNER OF THE CEMETERY AT ERZEROUM.

stained with the blood of the dead, presenting a fearful sight. The faces of many were disfigured beyond recognition, and all had been thrown down, face foremost, in the dust of the streets and mud of the gutters, so that all were black with clotted blood and dust. Some were stark naked, and every body seemed to have at least two wounds, and some a dozen. In this list of dead there were only three women, two babies, a number of young children, and about thirty young boys of fifteen to twenty. . . . Some Armenian workmen were engaged excavating a deep trench, twenty feet square, close by, to bury the corpses, and on one side were a number of skulls, perhaps twenty in all, and a pile of bones found in the excavating. I left the sad sight sick at heart."

Even at Constantinople itself, under the very shadow of the palace of the Sultan, the same spirit of massacre broke out. A perfectly peaceful demonstration on the part of the Armenians was treated as an outbreak of rebellion, and a hundred and seventy-two unfortunates were deliberately slain. Had it not been for the energetic attitude of the Ambassadors of the Great Powers, the policy of extermination would doubtless have been carried out to a far wider extent.

Of course the example of the capital found speedy imitation in the provinces of Asia Minor.

"I have just been reading," wrote the Constantinople correspondent of the *Speaker*, on 28th December, "some private letters, from three different towns, from ladies who were eyewitnesses of what they describe. They have been shut up for weeks in the midst of it, in constant danger of death themselves—their own windows riddled with bullets, and their rooms dark with the smoke of burning houses. They saw the soldiers shoot down helpless men and women, and then hack them to pieces with knives and swords; heads cut off and fixed on bayonets; little children disembowelled; women carried off to satisfy the lust of the soldiers; churches burned which were filled with men, women, and children; shops and houses stripped of everything, and the clothing taken from the backs of those not killed. They find themselves in the midst of thousands of people who are dying from day to day from terror, wounds, and starvation, and hear of the fate of their friends—this man flayed alive in the presence of his wife, this man brought in with his wife before the officials, and both of them shot because they refused to become Moslems; most of their friends among the young women carried off by force, declared Moslem, and given over to the harems of Turks; in one case all the women of a neighbouring village throwing themselves into the river to escape this fate. There is nothing sensational in the tone of these letters, as might be supposed from my grouping together of those facts. They tell the simple story of what they saw and heard each day. In all of them it is made clear that there will be very few Christians left in the spring. The Turks are doing their work with diabolical thoroughness."

Last winter the British Vice-Consul at Van described the condition of the Armenians in that city as too appallingly terrible for description. All through the fearful severity of the weather, women and girls were wandering in the snow-piled streets without shelter or food. They were barefoot, and in many cases they had been stripped of every garment but a chemise, and some had been left with but a mere rag to cover their nakedness.

Early in October 1895 a sudden massacre broke out at Trebizond. From eleven in the morning till six in the evening, the Turks rushed about the town murdering the Armenians and looting their houses. About six hundred were ruthlessly slain in one day, and for some weeks disorder prevailed, until the

sudden appearance of a Russian warship in the harbour brought the officials to their senses.

One example of the horrors perpetrated on this occasion may be given. An Armenian, coming out of a baker's shop where he had been purchasing bread for his sick wife, was seized by the Turks and dashed to the ground. First they cut off one of his hands, and placed it between his quivering lips. Soon afterwards they chopped off the other hand, and asked him if he wanted a pen to write to his wife. Some invited him to make the sign of the cross with his stumps, and others urged him to shout louder so that his God might hear. Next his ears were torn off and thrust into his mouth. "This Effendi's mouth deserves to be punished for refusing such a choice morsel," shouted one ruffian, who proceeded to knock out some of his teeth, and then cut out his tongue, with the remark, "He will never blaspheme again." After gouging out his eyes and cutting off his feet, they indulged in a few indescribable tortures, before cutting their victim's throat and sending his soul to damnation, as they expressed it. And all this was done by Moslem fanatics " in the Name of Allah, the Compassionate, the Merciful " !

Side by side with enormities such as these, the work of forced conversion has gone merrily on. The reports of Vice-Consul Fitzmaurice, published as lately as June 1896, have proved that the terrible alternative of Islam or death has been continually placed before the Armenian Christians. In many cases hundreds have been forced at the point of the sword to yield a nominal assent to the formula of Mohammedanism, to be circumcised, to adopt Turkish names, to turn their churches into mosques, and to outwardly practise the rites of Islam.

"Yet there are many," writes the Constantinople correspondent of the *Daily News*, " who elect to die martyrs for their faith. At Marash an Armenian, an ordained clergyman of the English Church, was offered the choice. He elected death, and was killed with slow torture. At Kharput, two Protestant preachers and a Syrian priest were murdered for the same cause. At Ichme, a number of Armenians had sought refuge in the Gregorian church. They were taken out one by one and asked to choose. Fifty-two died martyrs, the aged Protestant Pastor Krikor being among the first butchered. At Ouzoon, not far from Ichme, on the far bank of the Euphrates, a large number of Armenians were captured and led towards the neighbouring Turkish village to be compelled to change their faith. At a point where the road follows the river-bank, fifty-five of them rushed into the water and were drowned, rather than deny their religion, the Turks shooting at them the while. At Hoh, eighty-five were killed in this way. Their wives and daughters were taken into Moslem houses."

To record the atrocities which took place at the close of last year (1895) would be impossible within the limits of the present volume. The Blue Book (Turkey, No. 2—1896) which deals with the subject is a solid volume of 340 pages, and is simply lurid with horrors. Practically every Armenian town and village was treated in similar fashion; massacres, looting, and forced conversions were the normal state of affairs, and the policy of extermination was seen in full activity. The following details are condensed from the recent reports of Vice-Consul Fitzmaurice (Parliamentary Paper, Turkey, No. 5—1896):—

"On the 1st January 1896 (N.S.), at about 9 A.M., a general attack was made on the Christian quarter at Birejik. The assailants, armed with firearms, axes, hatchets, and similar weapons, were divided into three parties, one to break in the doors and walls, the second to plunder, and the third to massacre all males above a certain age. Every house in the Christian quarter was pillaged, the mob in their frenzy burning and destroying what they could not carry off; the ruin and desecration of the Gregorian, Catholic, and Protestant churches being carried out with special thoroughness. The carnage lasted till close on sunset, by which time over 150 Christians (I have in my possession a carefully checked list of their names) were massacred and over 60 wounded.

"The gloom of the sad events which had occurred during the last two months of 1895 at Ourfa, where I arrived on the 10th March, still hung over the town; and the Armenian quarter especially, in spite of attempts during the preceding ten weeks to remove the traces of the final disaster, still wore the aspect of a town which had been ruined and laid waste by some scourge more terrible than any war or siege. The shops, with their windows and doors broken in, lay empty and deserted; practically no grown males were visible; and only a few ill-clad and ill-fed children and women, with a scared look on their faces, were to be seen moving about, apparently in search of the bare necessities of existence in the shape of dry bread and scanty bedding.

"There have been two massacres at Ourfa, the first on 28th and 29th October 1895, and the second or big massacre on the 28th and 29th December of the same year. On the second occasion occurred an act which for fiendish barbarity has been unsurpassed by any of the horrors of recent massacres of Armenians, and for which the annals of history can furnish few, if any, parallels.

"On Saturday night, crowds of Armenian men, women, and children took refuge in their fine cathedral, capable of holding some eight thousand persons, and the priest administered the sacrament—the last sacrament, as it proved to be—to eighteen hundred souls, recording the figure on one of the pillars of the church. These remained in the cathedral over night, and were joined on Sunday by several hundreds more, who sought the protection of a building which they considered safe from mob-violence. It is computed that at least three thousand individuals were congregated in the edifice when the mob attacked it.

"They at first fired in through the windows, then smashed in the iron door, and proceeded to massacre all those, mostly men, who were on the ground floor. Having thus disposed of the men, and having removed some of the younger women, they rifled the church treasure, shrines, and ornaments, to the extent of some £T.4000; destroying the pictures and relics, mockingly calling on Christ now to prove Himself a greater prophet than Mohammed.

"A huge, partly stone, partly wooden gallery, running round the upper portion of the cathedral, was packed with a shrieking and terrified mass of women, children, and some men. Some of the mob, jumping on the raised altar platform, began picking off the latter with revolver shots, but as this process seemed too tedious, they bethought themselves of a more expeditious method. Having collected a quantity of bedding and the church matting, they poured some thirty cans of kerosene on it, as also on the dead bodies lying about, and then set fire to the whole. The gallery beams and wooden framework soon caught fire, whereupon, blocking up the staircases leading to the gallery with similar inflammable materials, they left the mass of struggling human beings to become the prey of the flames.

"During several hours the sickening smell of roasting flesh pervaded the town; and even to-day, two months and a half after the massacre, the smell of putrescent and charred remains in the church is unbearable.

"After very minute and careful inquiry, I believe that close on 8000 Armenians perished in the two days' massacre of the 28th and 29th December 1895, between 2500 and 3000 of whom were killed or burned in the cathedral."

It will be remembered that in addition to those who have thus been ruthlessly murdered, many hundreds of Armenians, whose only crimes were their Christianity and their wealth, have been thrown into prisons which exceed in horror even the most gruesome mediaeval conceptions of the nether world, and there tortured and starved until they found release either by death or by the delivery of all their property. What these prisons are may best be imagined by a description written last year by four Armenians [1]—one of them a clergyman—confined on a charge of sedition in Bitlis jail. Their letter is dated from "Bitlis Prison, *Hell,* March 28, 1895," and contains descriptions of such awful and bestial outrages that it is impossible to make public its worst parts. We give only those portions which are capable of translation into the language of decent and civilised people:—

"In Bitlis Prison there are seven cells, each one capable of containing from ten to twelve persons. The number they actually contain is from twenty to thirty. *There are no sanitary arrangements whatever.* Offal, vermin, and the filth that should find a special place elsewhere, are heaped together in the same cell. . . . The water is undrinkable. Frequently the Armenian prisoners are forced to drink 'khwlitsh' water—*i.e.* water from the tank in which the Mohammedans perform their ablutions. . . . Malkhass Aghadjanian and Serop Malkhassian of Avzoot (Moush) were beaten till they lost conscious-

---

[1] The names are in the possession of the Foreign Office; but they cannot be published, for obvious reasons.

ness. The former was branded in eight places, the latter in twelve places, with a hot iron. . . . Hagop Seropian, of the village of Avzoot, was stripped and beaten till he lost consciousness, then a girdle was thrown round his neck, and having been dragged into the Zaptieh's room, he was branded in sixteen parts of his body with red-hot ramrods. His hair was plucked out, he was made to stand motionless till nature could hold out no longer. . . . Sirko Minassian, Garabed Malkhassian, and Isro Ardvadzadoorian of the same village, having been violently beaten, were forced to remain in a standing position for a long time, and then had the contents of certain vessels poured upon their heads. Korki Mardoyan, of the village of Semal, was violently beaten; his hair was plucked out by the roots, and he was forced to stand motionless for twenty-four hours, . . . which resulted in his death. He was forty-five years of age. Mekhitar Saforian and Khatsho Baloyan of Kakarloo (Boolanyk) were subjected to the same treatment. *Mekhitar was but fifteen, and Khatsho only thirteen years old.* Sogho Sharoyan of Alvarindj (Moush) was conveyed from Moush to Bitlis prison handcuffed. Here he was cruelly beaten, and forced to maintain a standing position without food. Whenever he fainted they revived him with douches of cold water and stripes. They also plucked out his hair, and burned his body with red-hot irons. . . . Hambartzoon Boyadjian, after his arrest, was exposed to the scorching heat of the sun for three days. Then he was taken to Semal, where he and his companions were beaten and shut up in a church. They were not only not allowed to leave the church to relieve the wants of nature, but were forced to defile the baptismal font and the church altar. . . . Where are you, Christian England and America?"

In the words of Dr. Dillon, who is personally acquainted with these prisons, and has interviewed scores of persons who have passed through them: "The stories they relate of their experience there are gruesome, and would be hard to believe were they not amply confirmed by the still more eerie tales told by their broken spirits, their wasted bodies, and the deep scars and monstrous deformities that will abide with them till the grave or the vultures devour them. There is something so forbiddingly fantastic and wildly grotesque in the tortures and outrages invented by their jailers or their local governors, that a simple, unvarnished account of them sounds like the ravings of a diseased devil. But this is a subject upon which it is impossible to be explicit."

The most sickening horrors of the Inquisition, and the infamous persecutions of a Nero or a Diocletian, fade into insignificance beside the nameless outrages and the fiendish cruelties which are *now* being perpetrated from day to day upon Christian men, women, and children, by officials specially decorated and honoured by the unscrupulous and perjured despot who blasphemously calls himself, "The shadow of God upon Earth." Can we wonder when we hear that a weeping Armenian woman came to a missionary and asked the question, "Has God gone mad?"

To sum up this chapter of horrors. At the commencement of the present year (1896) a Committee of Delegates of the six Embassies at Constantinople drew up an official record of the outrages perpetrated upon the Armenians during the latter half of 1895. Omitting all statements which could not be proved to be accurate, the report gives details of the massacre of 25,000 Armenian Christians during those few months, and estimates that if the massacres respecting which there are no accurate figures were added to these, a sum total of probably 30,000 would be reached. The list will be found in Blue Book, Turkey, No 2—1896.

The British Ambassador thus summarises the whole account: "It may be roughly stated that the recent disturbances have devastated, as far as the Armenians are concerned, the whole of the provinces to which the scheme of reforms was intended to apply; that over an extent of territory considerably larger than Great Britain, all the large towns, with the exception of Van, Samsoun, and Moush, have been the scene of massacres of the Armenian population, while the Armenian villages have been almost entirely destroyed. A moderate estimate puts the loss of life at 30,000. The survivors are in a state of absolute destitution, and in many places they are forced to turn Mussulman. The charge against the Armenians of having been the first to offer provocation cannot be sustained. The participation of the soldiers in the massacres is in many places established beyond doubt."

CHAPTER VIII.

EUROPE'S RESPONSIBILITY.

THE preceding chapters have probably proved sufficiently gruesome reading, and it is time to ask ourselves if nothing can be done to stop, effectually and finally, the atrocities which for many months past have disgraced the Ottoman Government, and have outraged the sensibilities of the entire civilised world.

A cheap and easy method with appeals and protests from Armenia, is to reply that, however deplorable the internal management of Turkey may be, it is no concern of ours, and that we are not entitled to meddle with another nation's business. Such an answer to the appeals of outraged women and orphaned children is not one which should commend itself to a people claiming to be both Christian and civilised. The policy of non-interference becomes both cowardly and criminal in the presence of unspeakable wrong. If it be unmanly and shameful to stand idly by while one single act of barbarity is committed, surely indifference in the presence of such fiendish enormities as we have described becomes infinitely despicable. The cause of humanity and of Christianity is far too sacred to be fettered by the red tapeism of diplomatic etiquette. There is a righteousness which exalteth a nation, and never was resolute intervention more truly an act of national righteousness than here. We are not unmindful of the horrors of war, and of the grave responsibility resting upon any man who opens the floodgates of international carnage; but war is not the supreme evil. There is a heavier calamity which may befall; it is—NATIONAL DISGRACE. It may safely be predicted that when the Armenian question is viewed in its true perspective at the distance of say fifty future years, there will be found few to dispute that the nations of Europe covered themselves with shame, when by political jealousies and diplomatic triflings they suffered opportunity to slip by, and left the wretched Armenians to a fate worse than death. The plea that we should mind our own business is but the paltry subterfuge of a small and ignoble spirit when the higher dictates of justice and humanity call loudly for interference.

But there is much more than this to be said. *The Armenian question is our business.* The Ottoman Empire exists to-day, and tortures and murders its Christian subjects, by virtue of British intervention and on the strength of British guarantees. Both in 1853 and again in 1878 we interfered to save it. But for us, "the shadow of God" would long since have been swept out of Europe. We fought for the Turk, we financed the Turk with British gold, we supplied him with ships, we dragged the Great Powers of Europe into treaties with him, and generally saved him from the Nemesis which followed hard upon his crimes. In return, we wrested from him promises that he would reform, and undertook the responsibility of compelling him to carry out his pledges. Again and again we have been his sponsors at the bar of Europe, and we need to look to it lest we be called upon to answer for his misdeeds before a still higher tribunal.

In the words of the Duke of Argyll: "It is not too much to say that England has twice saved Turkey from complete subjection since 1853. It is largely—mainly—due to our action that she now exists at all as an independent Power. On both occasions we dragged the Powers of Europe along with us in maintaining the Ottoman Government. On both occasions we did so avowedly, and on the last occasion expressly, on the ground that we—Europe—would undertake that protectorate over the Christian subjects of the Sultan which Russia sought to establish in her own hands alone. We are bound by every consideration of duty and honour to do our very utmost to discharge so solemn and so tremendous an obligation. It is one which does not arise only, or even mainly, out of general considerations of humanity. It arises out of our own decided and repeated action in keeping up what is now seen to be a Government which is weak, cruel, and corrupt."

Let us briefly pass in review the treaties which not only permit, but demand, our interference at the present crisis. At the close of the Crimean War, in 1856, the Treaty of Paris, which aimed "to secure, through effectual and reciprocal guarantees, the independence and integrity of the Ottoman Empire," did not sanction any outside interference in the internal affairs of Turkey. But the Protocol of London, under date 31st March 1877, says: "The Powers that have undertaken to pacify the East recognise that the surest means of attaining the object they have set before them is, above all, to maintain the understanding so happily existing among them, and to jointly reaffirm the common interest which they take in the promotion of the rights of the Christian populations of Turkey." In the event of reforms not being carried out, the Protocol goes on to say that "they think it their duty to declare that such a state of things would be incompatible with their interests, and those of Europe in general. In such a contingency they reserve to themselves the joint consideration of the means they consider the best adapted to assure the welfare of the Christian populations and the interests of general peace."

At the close of the Russo-Turkish War in 1878, came the Treaty of San Stefano, the 16th Article of which runs as follows: "As the evacuation by the Russian troops of the territory which they occupy in Armenia, and which is to be restored to Turkey, might give rise to conflicts and complications detrimental to the maintenance of good relations between the two countries, the Sublime Porte engages to carry into effect, *without further delay*, the improvements and reforms demanded by local requirements in the provinces inhabited by the Armenians, and to guarantee their security from Kurds and Circassians."

On 30th May 1878 a memorandum was signed in London by Lord Salisbury and Count Schouvaloff, which stated, *inter alia*: "The promises respecting Armenia stipulated in the preliminary Treaty of San Stefano, must not be made exclusively to Russia, but to England also."

Next came the Cyprus Treaty, of 4th June 1878, in which Turkey promised "to introduce necessary reforms, to be agreed upon later between the two Powers, into the government and for the protection of the Christian and other subjects of the Porte, in these territories," and handed over Cyprus as a pledge of good faith.

In the same year the Treaty of Berlin was signed, the 61st Article of which is as follows:—

"The Sublime Porte engages to realise, *without delay*, those ameliorations and reforms which local needs require in the provinces inhabited by the Armenians, and to guarantee their security against the Circassians and the Kurds. It undertakes to make known from time to time the measures taken

SIR PHILIP CURRIE, C.M.G.,
BRITISH AMBASSADOR AT CONSTANTINOPLE.
(Photo by Russell.)

with this object to the Powers, *who will watch over their application.*"

In this connection, the 62nd Article should also be carefully noted:—

"The Sublime Porte having expressed the intention to maintain the principle of religious liberty, and give it the widest scope, the contracting parties take note of this spontaneous declaration.

"In no part of the Ottoman Empire shall difference of religion be alleged against any person as a ground for exclusion or incapacity as regards the discharge of civil and political rights, admission to the public employments, functions, and honours, or the exercise of the various professions and industries.

"All persons shall be admitted, without distinction of religion, to give evidence before the tribunals.

"The freedom and outward exercise of all forms of worship are assured to all, and no hindrance shall be offered either to the hierarchical organisations of the various communions or to their relations with their spiritual chiefs."

In view of these repeated pledges, it is not too much to say that the Ottoman Government now stands before the world convicted of deliberate and repeated perjury. But what about the other parties to these treaties? They surely pledged themselves to see these promises fulfilled, and, in the words of the Treaty of Berlin, "to watch over their application." The British flag still flies in the island of Cyprus, a silent witness to the contract by which we pledged ourselves that Turkish reforms should be carried out.

What, then, has Europe done in the present crisis? Perhaps the best reply will be found in the speech of Professor Bryce to his constituents at Aberdeen on 21st January 1896:—

"There is a still more painful subject on which I

must speak freely to you. For many years in succession I have described to you the sufferings of the Armenian Christians, have pointed out England's responsibilities, and have repeated to you the predictions of persons who knew the East thoroughly, that before long some massacre would ensue sufficient to endanger the peace of the whole East and so compel the intervention of the European Powers. Those predictions have been only too completely fulfilled. The massacre of Sassoun—an unprovoked massacre, and part of a deliberate scheme for the extermination of the Christian population—was perpetrated on a community of simple mountaineers, the flower of what remained of the Armenian race. Lord Rosebery's Government spoke to the Sultan in the very strongest terms, pressing the need for prompt and sweeping reforms, and for the punishment of the guilty; and they endeavoured to get Russia and France to join with them. The Turks, of course, resisted, never expressing the slightest regret or remorse for the slaughter, while Russia and France gave a somewhat qualified support, hesitating to adopt what we thought even the irreducible minimum of reforms. We were still arguing with them and pressing the Sultan when we quitted office last June. The time had not then yet arrived for proceeding to coerce the Turks,—though it was plain that it must soon have arrived,—because it was deemed proper first to exhaust the resources of remonstrance and warning, and if possible, to carry Russia and France along with us. When Parliament opened last August, Lord Salisbury addressed to the Turks grave words, which were taken by the country as a pledge that England would do everything she could to secure protection for the Eastern Christians. He repeated this pledge in still stronger and clearer terms in his Guildhall speech. By that time fresh massacres had begun. Massacres have gone on ever since. They have been secretly planned or publicly organised by the Turkish Government, and either permitted or actually carried out by Turkish troops. Tens of thousands of Christians have been slain. Probably as many more have been made homeless, and are dying of famine. Some have sought to escape death by renouncing their religion. . . .

"And while these things go on, Britain does nothing. Sir Michael Hicks-Beach says we have no special responsibility, forgetting the Anglo-Turkish Convention, forgetting that it was England that set aside the Treaty of San Stefano, by which Russia had undertaken to protect the Armenians, and Britain that substituted for that treaty the Treaty of Berlin, by whose 61st Article our obligation stands plainly written; and Mr. Arthur Balfour, while deploring the position, offers no consolation except that 'The Concert of Europe has been maintained.' Six Powers, any one of which could, by moving a few ironclads, bring the Turk to his knees and stop the massacres, stand helplessly while massacres go on far worse than those which desolated Armenia in the twelfth century, or in those later days when the Turk, now so feeble except for massacre, was the terror of all Christendom. The Concert of Europe is maintained! Six strong men stand by while a ruffian tortures and despatches the victim they have pledged themselves to protect. And it is owing to Britain more than to any other Power that the Turkish Government has lived on to do its hideous work, for it was Britain that saved that Government in the days of the Crimean War—Britain that in 1878 deprived the Armenians of the protection which Russia had then promised. So now Britain is bound above all the other Powers to come to the rescue of these victims of ferocity and fanaticism."

There can be little doubt, as Canon MacColl has

clearly pointed out, that the British Government made four great blunders in dealing with the recent outrages in Armenia. In the first instance, it was an undoubted mistake to suppress the consular reports from Asia Minor, and so lead the Sultan to suppose that we wished to screen him from the indignation of Europe. Then it was a grave mistake to accept, and so far accredit, the Turkish Commission of Inquiry, which was from first to last an impudent imposture. The third blunder was "to present a scheme of reforms so elaborate and complex as to delight the hearts of the Sultan and his pashas for the opportunity which it gave for endless discussion, and so entirely inadequate as to be perfectly futile"; and to crown it all, this scheme was presented in so tentative and hesitating a fashion, that the Sultan treated it with something very like contempt.

"There is only one effectual way of dealing with a Sultan of Turkey in a matter of this sort. Make up your mind what you want; put your demand into the shortest and clearest form possible; and then demand an answer, without discussion, within a given time, with an intimation of coercion in case of refusal: and if the Sultan sees that you mean it, he will yield without more ado."

It is much to be regretted that the eloquent voice which rang throughout England in 1876, and roused the nations of Europe to indignation at the Bulgarian atrocities, should now be comparatively silenced through extreme age. But Mr. Gladstone's testimony has not been altogether lacking in the parallel circumstances of these past months. At the close of 1894, when the first rumours of the Sassoun massacre reached England, Mr. Gladstone delivered the following stirring words in the course of an address to a deputation from the National Church of Armenia:—

"The intelligence which has reached me tends to a

conclusion which I still hope may not be verified, but tends strongly to a conclusion to the general effect that the outrages and the scenes and abominations of 1876 in Bulgaria have been repeated in 1894 in Armenia. As I have said, I hope it is not so, and I will hope to the last; but if it is so, *it is time that one general shout of execration directed against deeds of wickedness should rise from outraged humanity*, and should force itself into the ears of the Sultan of Turkey, and make him sensible, if anything can make him sensible, of the madness of such a course. . . .

"I have lived to see the Empire of Turkey in Europe reduced to less than one half of what it was when I was born, and why? Simply because of its misdeeds—a great record written by the hand of Almighty God, in whom the Turk, as a Mohammedan, believes, and believes firmly—written by the hand of Almighty God against injustice, against lust, against the most abominable cruelty; and if happily—I am hoping against hope—if the reports we have read are to be disproved or to be mitigated, then let us thank God; but if, on the other hand, they be established, then I say it will more than ever stand before the world that there is no lesson, however severe, that can teach certain people the duty, the prudence, the necessity of observing in some degree the laws of decency, and of humanity, and of justice, and that if allegations such as these are established, it will stand as if it were written with letters of iron on the records of the world, that such a Government as that which can countenance and cover the perpetration of such outrages is a disgrace in the first place to Mohammed, the Prophet whom it professes to follow, that it is a disgrace to civilisation at large, and that it is a curse to mankind.

"Now, this is strong language. Strong language

ought to be used when facts are strong, and ought not to be used without strength of facts."

We add an extract from Mr. Gladstone's famous paper, entitled *Bulgarian Horrors and the Question of the East*, which is so entirely pertinent to the present occasion that we have ventured to substitute the word Armenia for Bulgaria:—

"I entreat my countrymen, upon whom far more than perhaps any other people of Europe it depends, to require and to insist that our Government, which has been working in one direction, shall work in the other, and shall apply all its vigour to concur with the other States of Europe in obtaining the extinction of the Turkish executive power in Armenia. Let the Turks now carry away their abuses in the only possible manner—namely, by carrying off themselves. Their Zaptiehs and their Mudirs, their Bimbashis and their Yuzbachis, their Kaimakans and their Pashas—one and all, bag and baggage—shall, I hope, clear out from the province they have desolated and profaned. This thorough riddance, this most blessed deliverance, is the only reparation we can make to the memory of those heaps on heaps of dead; to the violated purity alike of matron, of maiden, and of child; to the civilisation which has been affronted and shamed; to the laws of God, or, if you like, of Allah; to the moral sense of mankind at large. There is not a criminal in a European jail, there is not a cannibal in the South Sea Islands, whose indignation would not arise and overboil at the recital of that which has been done; which has too late been examined, but which remains unavenged; which has left behind it all the foul and all the fierce passions that produced it: and which may again spring up, in another murderous harvest, from the soil soaked and reeking with blood, and in the air tainted with every imaginable deed of crime and shame. *That such things should be done once is a damning disgrace to the portion of our race which did them; that a door should be left open for their ever-so-barely possible repetition would spread that shame over the whole.* Better, we may justly tell the Sultan, almost any inconvenience, difficulty, or loss associated with Armenia—

> 'Than thou reseated in thy place of light,
> The mockery of thy people and their bane.'

"We may ransack the annals of the world; but I know not what research can furnish us with so portentous an example of the fiendish misuse of the powers established by God, 'for the punishment of evil-doers, and for the encouragement of them that do well.' No Government ever has so sinned; none has so proved itself incorrigible in sin, or, which is the same, so impotent for reformation."

These are wholesome words, and it were well if they could be widely echoed through the land. But words are of little use unless they bear fruit in action. No mere words will heal the gaping wounds of Armenia. Even while we pen these closing lines, there come tidings that another massacre has taken place, in which some three hundred and forty Armenians were barbarously slain. The villages still lie in blackened ruins, women and children are still wandering, homeless, ill-clad, and starving, amongst the mountains, and the much-vaunted scheme of reform has resulted in practically nothing.

Diplomacy has conspicuously failed; it is time that the Christian feeling of the nations found expression, not in words but in deeds. To still stand idly by, and talk vain platitudes in pulpit and on platform, while all the time the vultures hover in the tainted air, and feast upon the mutilated bodies of men and women, whose only crime was faith in Christ, is to act the coward's part.

> "Lo! from a land that pleads
> For mercy where no mercy is, the ghosts
> Look in upon you faltering at your posts—
> Upbraid you parleying while a People bleeds
> To death."

It is time that Europe, and England most of all, struck an effectual blow at the loathsome tyranny, the intolerable misgovernment which has transformed an old-time paradise into a veritable hell. The blood of Armenia's slaughtered sons and daughters cries aloud to God and man for vengeance!

APPENDIX.

HISTORY moves slowly in Turkey when it is a question of instituting reforms, but fast enough when massacres are in the air. Within a few days of the publication of the first edition of this book, the whole Armenian question was suddenly reopened by the perpetration, *on European soil*, of a wholesale slaughter of inoffensive people, on a scale equal to any of the massacres which have recently taken place in Asia Minor.

On Wednesday, 26th August 1896, occurred an incident which was made the excuse for turning Stamboul, the fairest city of the East, into a veritable shambles. Following the rule laid down in the Preface, we confine ourselves to those facts which have been reported from sources of unquestionable veracity, and we are largely indebted to *The Times* newspaper for the details which follow.

The representatives of an Armenian Patriotic Society, most of whose members reside at Van, presented a memorial to the Porte and to the European Embassies on Tuesday, 25th August, in which they stated that they were reduced to utter despair, and that to avoid a disaster the promised scheme of reforms must be made operative at once. To give strength to this document, they planned a most foolish and disastrous demonstration. The idea seems to have been to lodge dynamite in the cellars of the Ottoman Bank, occupy the building by force, and then threaten to blow up the entire premises unless they received a promise that the needed reforms should be carried out. Accordingly, about noon on the following day, some twenty-five members of the society, at a given signal, rushed into the bank, revolvers were fired, and three or four bombs were thrown and exploded in the vestibule, shattering all the glass, while others were thrown into the street.

The panic-stricken officials rushed upstairs, leaving some £10,000 at the mercy of the invaders, who touched not a farthing of it, but subsequently helped the cashier to lock it up in safety. For the remainder of the day, the employés of the Bank were held as hostages, while Sir Edgar Vincent and M. Maximoff, chief dragoman to the Russian Embassy, went to Yildiz to endeavour to make such arrangements with the authorities as would rid the bank of its unwelcome visitors. In the meantime the Turkish troops surrounded the premises, and a brisk fusilade was kept up.

About midnight the negotiators returned to the bank, and after a long parley it was arranged that Sir Edgar Vincent and M. Maximoff should guarantee the safety of the invaders on condition that they evacuated the bank. The troops then withdrew, the dynamite was removed, and the demonstrators were conveyed with an escort of gendarmes on board Sir E. Vincent's yacht at Kadileui, whence they sailed to Marseilles.

So far good, but a terrible tale remains to be told. In civilised countries it is the practice to punish the guilty and protect the innocent. But this is not the way they do things in Turkey. Where "the Shadow of God" darkens the earth, it is the custom to let the guilty escape, and to then vindicate the arm of the law by murdering the innocent.

No sooner had the attack upon the Ottoman Bank taken place than the streets were filled with an armed mob, which sprang into existence so promptly and set to work so systematically, that it is impossible to avoid the conclusion to which the diplomatic witnesses came, that it was previously organised. Armed with yataghans and iron-shod clubs, the mob set upon the Armenians of Constantinople and without discrimination brained and disembowelled them in the streets. Within two hours every street in the lower part of Galata was literally flowing with Christian blood. The troops were quickly on the scene to regulate the traffic, but never made the slightest attempt to check the murderous proceedings of the Mohammedan populace.

The afternoon and evening were devoted to scenes of carnage, and all through the night the mob took free vengeance on the Armenians, murdering, wrecking houses, and pillaging shops, while the authorities exercised no restraint upon them. The number of persons killed between Wednesday and Sunday is estimated by the Embassies at between five thousand and six thousand, largely belonging to the class of street porters. About a thousand more were missing. In some districts of Constantinople, scarcely a single male Armenian escaped the fury of the mob, while in one house forty-five women and children who had taken refuge on the roof were all murdered and their bodies thrown into the street. Several Armenians who sought refuge in foreign steamers were pursued by softas in boats and killed.

The disturbances were renewed on the following day, and not till two hours after sunset were orders given to the Bashi-Bazouks to cease the slaughter. *The massacre thus lasted thirty hours, during which time the troops and the police remained perfectly passive.* There could not possibly be more damning evidence than this that the slaughter was approved by the Sultan and his advisers. In the words of *The Times* newspaper—"Neither in diplomatic circles, nor in the minds of rational observers, does doubt exist that the armed Turkish mob which wrought the bloodshed had been previously organised for the purpose."

The troops did nothing but shelter the banded assassins from interference with their bloody work, insulting and roughly handling those who appealed to them to prevent it. The only place where the murderers encountered resistance was at Psamatia, where the Armenians fought in self-defence, till they came to their last cartridge. One young woman fought desperately in defence of her aged father, and died covered with wounds. Everywhere else the wretched Armenians seemed stupefied with terror, and were simply knocked on the head like rabbits: some ran for their lives, but were quickly hunted down by the mob. While the banded assassins slew every Armenian they could find, the police and gendarmes arrested all they could lay hands on. These poor wretches were pinioned and marched off, being cruelly beaten as they went, to one or other of the police depôts, which many entered only to be brought out to the dead-cart on the other side.

The following extract is taken from a private letter from a resident in Constantinople:—"From the bottom of our street to Azap Kapou, there were more than two hundred men killed, all Armenians. All their shops were smashed, and the contents stolen. I am not exaggerating in the least. In the night, as we were just going to bed, I heard revolver shots and cries. In the morning I inquired what had happened in the night. I was informed that the Sultan had given orders to murder all Armenians that could be got hold of, and that they were to pillage for twenty-four hours. In the quarter where I lived, there was not one Armenian left. I suppose that there were from ten to fifteen men. At the Armenian quarter, on the top of Hasskeui, there is not a single Armenian left. They say that five hundred men or more were killed. After the killing affair was finished, from our house I counted five carts full of bodies; they had been struck on the head, and their throats had been cut just like sheep. Empty carts were sent to our part, and forty-five went away full of dead bodies. They were taken over the hills: these carts were filled twice.

"The twenty-four hours are ended, and the murdering has abated a little in our part, because there are very few more Armenians left to be killed. The corpses were piled one on top of the other, just like sardines, close to our door. My hand is trembling with fright at the horrible things that I have seen. These poor Armenians were killed with large pieces of wood striking them on their heads, and after they were stunned, the Turks got large stones and smashed in their heads, after which they cut their throats."

So wholesale was the massacre, that it was found impossible to bury the dead in an adequate manner, and the state of the Chichli Cemetery is described as being scarcely endurable. When the slaughter ceased, the persecution by no means ended. Over three thousand Armenians were arrested, and without any specified accusation were thrown into prison. Wholesale deportation became the order of the day. The miserable creatures were driven like cattle to the quays and embarked on Turkish vessels, professedly destined for Asia Minor. The ugliest rumours are abroad as to the fate of these people. It is even stated that they were simply thrown into the sea: certainly nothing has—at the time of writing—been heard of them. If they have been really conveyed to Asia Minor, the scene of last year's atrocities, one can have little doubt of the true motives of their oppressors.

Now it may appear at first sight that the Constantinople massacre was simply an outbreak of ungovernable popular wrath on account of the insane and reprehensible attack on the Ottoman Bank. But it has been proved to the satisfaction of the representatives of the great European Powers that such was not the case. No graver charge could be brought against the Ottoman Government than is contained in the collective Note addressed to the Porte on August 31 by the Ambassadors of Austria, France, Germany, Italy, Russia, and Great Britain. It runs thus:—

"Referring to their collective Note of August 27, the representatives of the Great Powers believe it their duty to draw the attention of the Sublime Porte to an exceptionally serious side of the disorders which have recently stained with blood the capital and its environs. It is the declaration, on positive *data*, of the fact that the savage bands which murderously attacked the Armenians and pillaged the houses and shops which they entered under pretence of looking for agitators were not accidental gatherings of fanatical people, but presented every indication of a special organisation known by certain agents of the authorities, if not directed by them. This is proved by the following circumstances:—

"1. The bands rose simultaneously, at different points of the town, at the first news of the occupation of the bank by the Armenian revolutionaries, before even the police or an armed force had appeared on the scene of the disorder; while the Sublime Porte admits that information was received in advance by the police regarding the criminal designs of the agitators.

"2. A great part of the people who composed these bands were dressed and armed in the same manner.

"3. They were led or accompanied by softas, soldiers, or even police officers, who not only looked on unmoved at their excesses, but at times even took part in them.

"4. Several heads of the detective police were seen to distribute cudgels and knives among these Bashi-Bazouks, and point out to them the direction to take in search of victims.

"5. They were able to move about freely and accomplish their crimes with impunity under the eyes of the troops and their officers, even in the vicinity of the Imperial Palace.

"6. One of the assassins, arrested by the dragoman of one of the Embassies, declared that the soldiers could not arrest him. On being taken to Yildiz Palace, he was received by the attendants as one of their acquaintances.

"7. Two Turks employed by Europeans, who disappeared during the two days' massacre, declared on their return that they had been requisitioned and armed with knives and cudgels in order to kill Armenians."

The only reply to this most serious statement has been a bare denial on the part of the Sultan, who thus practically gives the lie to the Great Powers of Europe in the persons of their Ambassadors.

Considerations of space forbid us to enter at any length upon the attitude of England in the present crisis. When the first edition of this book appeared, —not three weeks ago,—Mr. Gladstone expressed the hope that the public might be aroused "to a due sense of the shame and infamy we are undergoing, in common with the people of other great States, at the hands of the Assassin who sits on the throne of Constantinople." That hope is now in a fair way to fulfilment. From end to end of the land a great cry of indignation and humiliation is going up. Pulpit and platform are unanimous in condemnation of a policy of time-serving indifference.

Even *The Times*—the last newspaper to be carried away by popular clamour—has recognised the fact. In its leader of 14th September, it speaks thus :—

"It has long been quite clear to all whose duty it is to watch the course of public opinion that upon this subject popular feeling is in a highly sensitive state. That is the natural, the inevitable, and the laudable result of the long series of detestable crimes which have constituted the recent internal history of portions of the Turkish Empire. The words used by Lord Rosebery, and by others who are less accustomed to measure the language they employ, are not one whit too strong as an expression of the sentiments experienced by Englishmen of all classes, all conditions, and all parties, as they have read the long record of inhuman cruelties perpetrated on the miserable Armenian race. The indignation of the British people is, as Lord Rosebery says, 'almost past the power of expression,' and he is doubtless right when he adds that it is aggravated by the appearance and perhaps the reality of impotence."

There can be no question that the Government will be strongly backed by popular sentiment in any effective action it may take to rescue the victims of Turkish savagery and to wipe off the stain which our national escutcheon has received. We are not advocating war,—God forbid!—but we do say that if England is compelled to once more unsheathe the sword, the heart of the nation will be found to beat strong and true as in days of old. May God defend the right!

PRINTED BY
MORRISON AND GIBB LIMITED, EDINBURGH.

www.ingramcontent.com/pod-product-compliance
Lightning Source LLC
Chambersburg PA
CBHW020130170426
43199CB00010B/714